Sampler Book 11, Ontario in Colour Photos, Saving Our History One Photo at a Time

Photography by Barbara Raué ©2019

Series Name: Sampler Cruising Ontario

Sampling from Durham County

Each photo I take that precedes a demolition, or a natural disaster such as a tornado or a fire, is meeting this aim of mine of Saving Our History One Photo at a Time. There are more than 100 towns already photographed which you can visit without moving from a comfortable chair in your living room.

©All the photos in this book have been taken with my cameras. I own the rights to them.

Cover: Bentley House, Brougham village, Page 35

Table of Contents

Whitby, Ontario – Book 1 - in Colour Photos – My Top 15 Picks

Whitby is located in Durham Region in Southern Ontario, east of Ajax and west of Oshawa, on the north shore of Lake Ontario. It is about twenty kilometers (twelve miles) east of the Toronto borough of Scarborough. The southern part of Whitby is predominantly urban and an economic hub; the northern part is more rural and includes the communities of Ashburn, Brooklin, Myrtle, and Myrtle Station.

Whitby was named after the seaport town of Whitby, Yorkshire, England. Settlement dates back to 1800, however, it was not until 1836 that a downtown business center was established by Whitby's founder Peter Perry. Whitby's chief asset was its natural harbor on Lake Ontario, from which grain from the farmland to the north was first shipped in 1833. In the 1840s, a road was built from Whitby Harbor to Lake Simcoe and Georgian Bay, to bring trade and settlement through the harbor to and from the rich land to the north.

Many residents commute to work in other Greater Toronto Area communities, and General Motors Canada in Oshawa is a major employer for all of Durham Region. Whitby has a steel mill, a retail support center operated by Sobeys, and a major Liquor Control Board of Ontario warehouse.

Four railways pass through Whitby. The Toronto-Montreal corridor main lines of the Canadian National Railway and Canadian Pacific Railway both pass east–west through the south end of town. A second CP line running from Toronto to Havelock passes through the northern part of Whitby. Via Rail trains travel through Whitby, but the nearest station is in Oshawa. GO Transit provides frequent service via its Lakeshore East line.

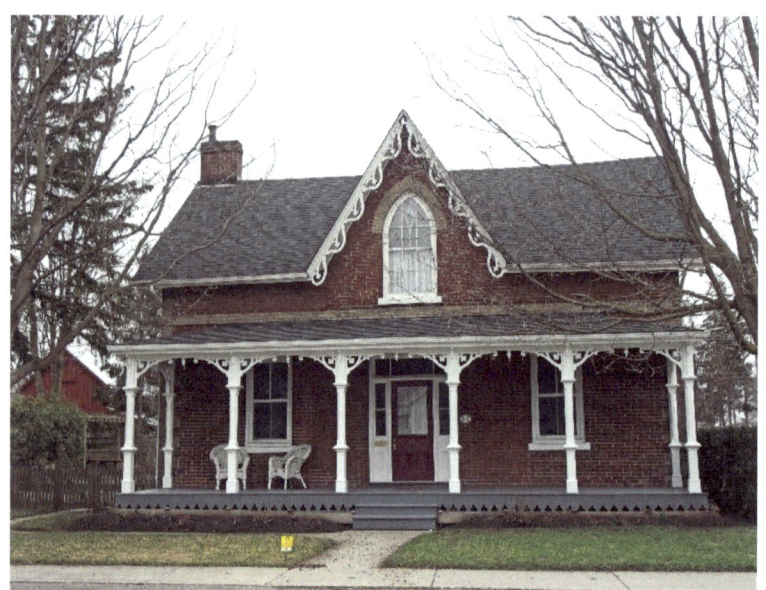

300 Centre Street South – Holden Jackson House – 1869

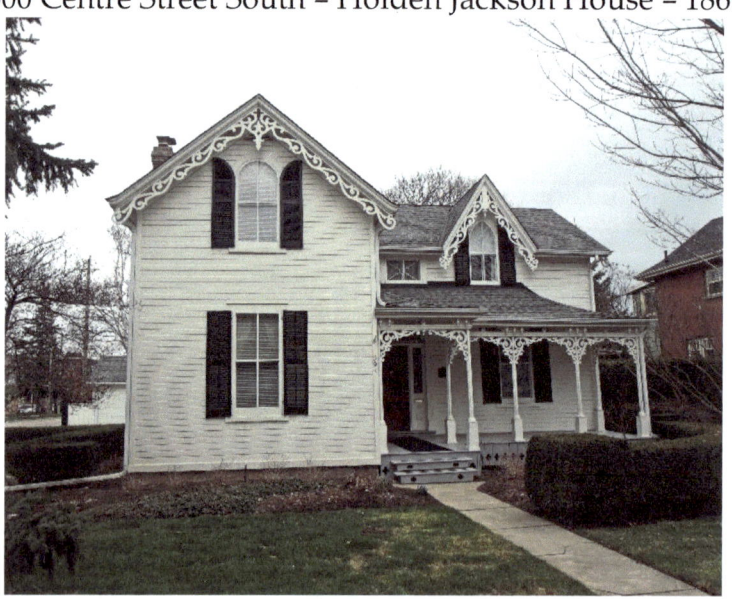

301 Centre Street South – c. 1875 – built for William Hood, a retired Whitby farmer and son of an English settler – rubble-stone foundation, white clapboard building, two-storey vernacular Gothic Revival

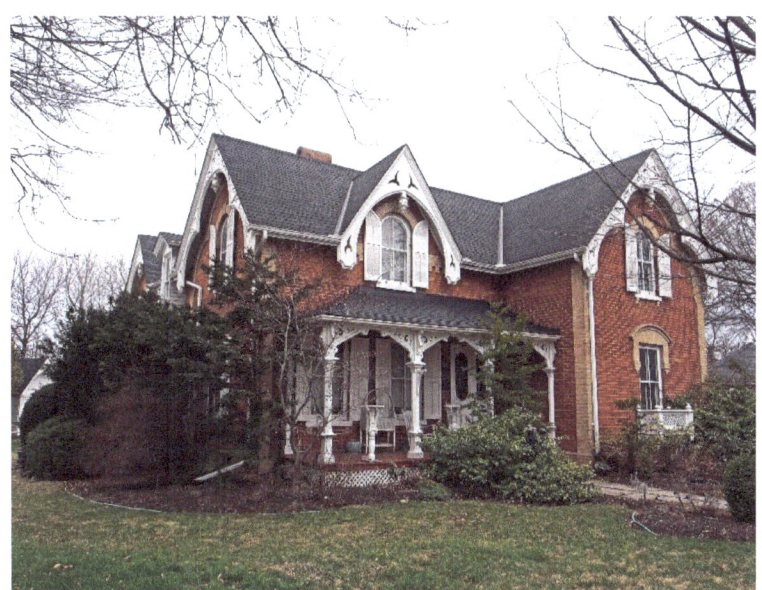

Centre Street South – bargeboard trim on gables, shutters

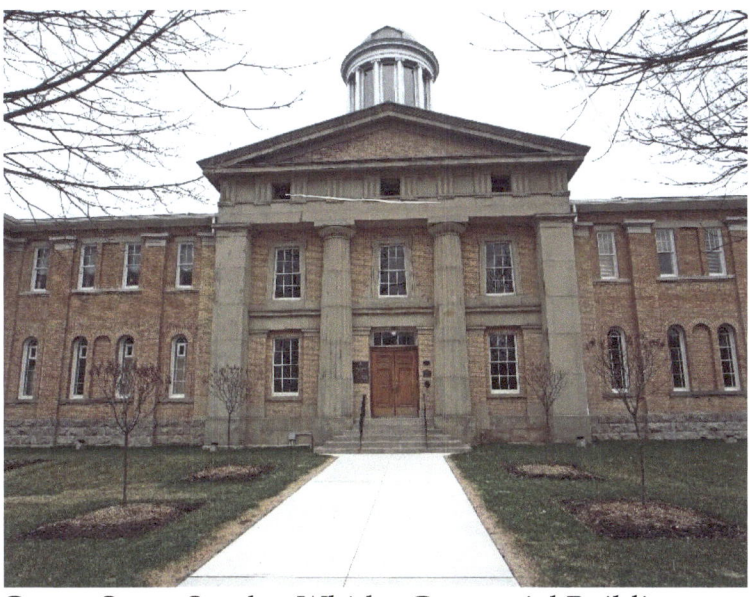

416 Centre Street South – Whitby Centennial Building was designed by Cumberland and Strom in the Greek Revival style. It was built in 1853 with the second floor added in 1910. It served as Ontario County Court House from 1854 to 1964.

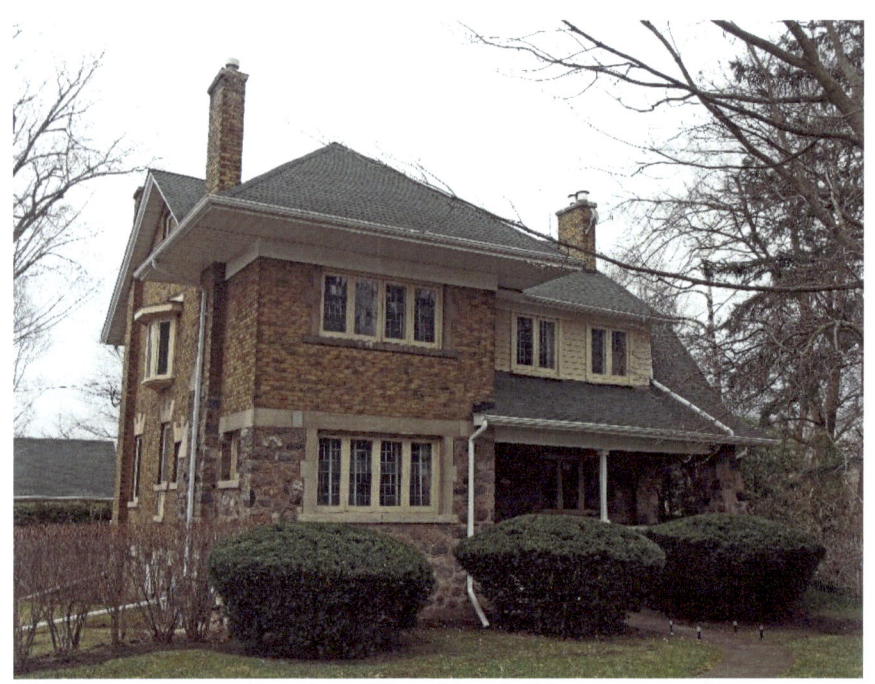

601 Centre Street South – Clive Hatch House - combines elements of the Prairie style architecture and Arts & Crafts style – c. 1915

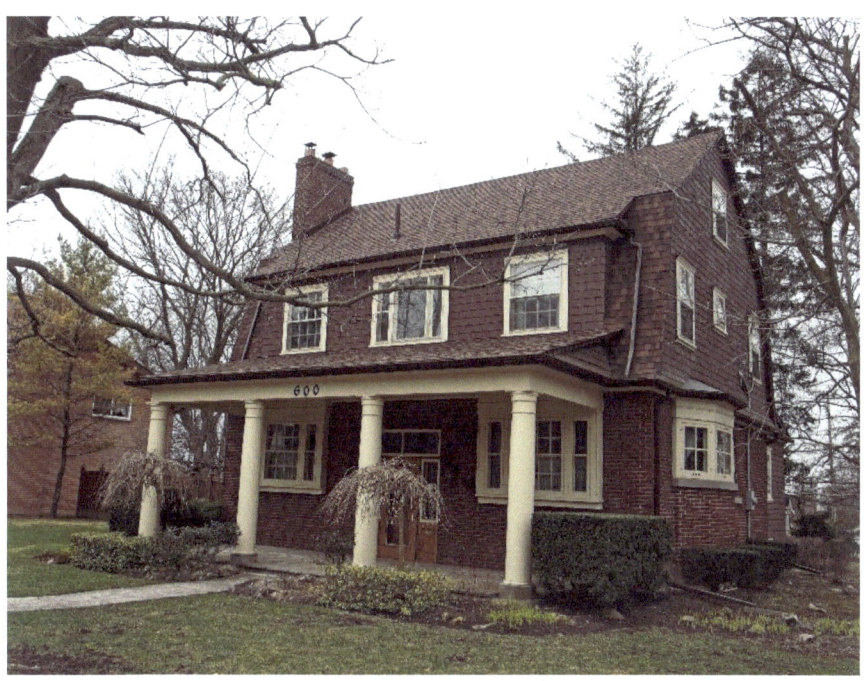

600 King Street – c. 1913 – gambrel roof – built for Dr. Horace Bascom who was Clerk of the Ontario County Court from 1912-55

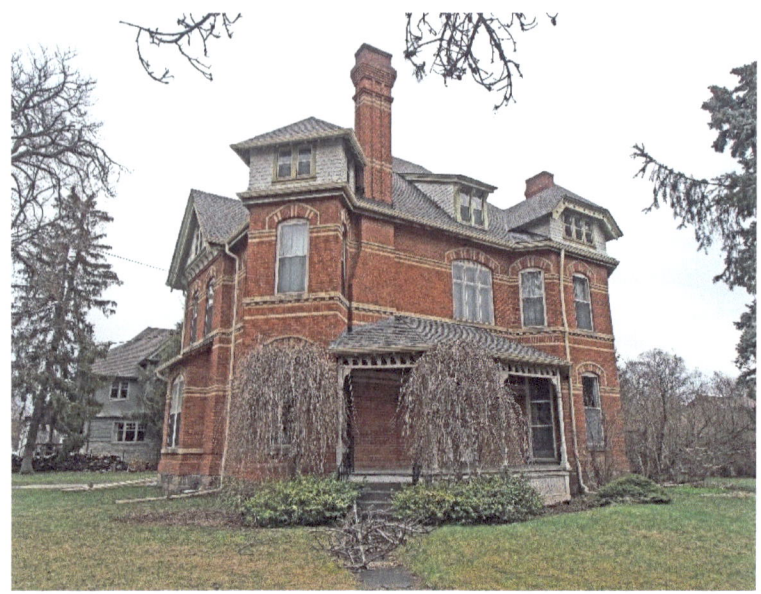

320 St. John Street West – c. 1881 – designed by Canadian architect, Henry Langley – high Victorian style – built for Judge George Dartnell – From 1899 to 1920, it was the home of Judge Duncan John McIntyre.

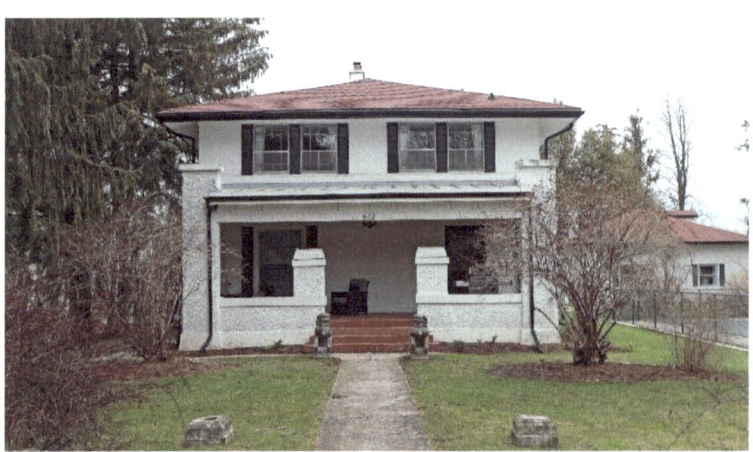

400 St. John Street West – c. 1913 – Prairie style – built for George Dryden, Registrar of Deeds for Ontario County from 1897 to 1931

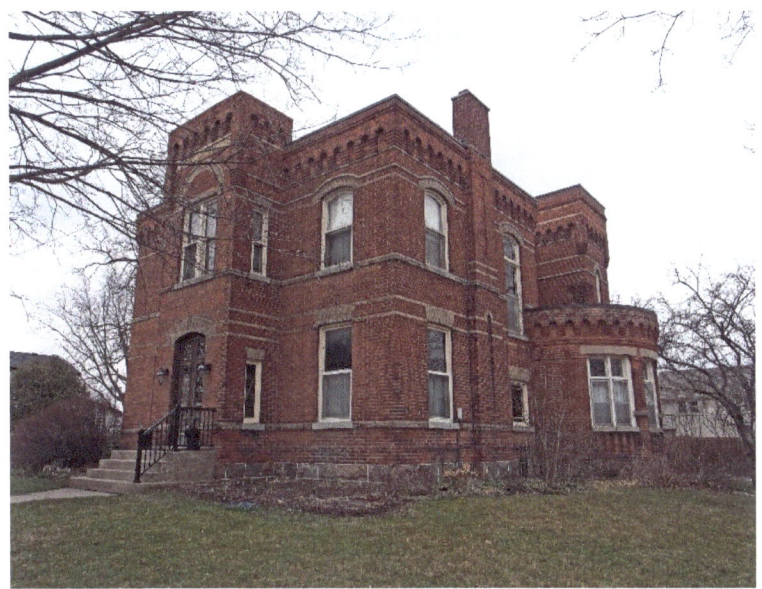

200 Colborne Street West - George Conrad Gross House –
Castle Style house built in Gothic Revival style - c. 1883

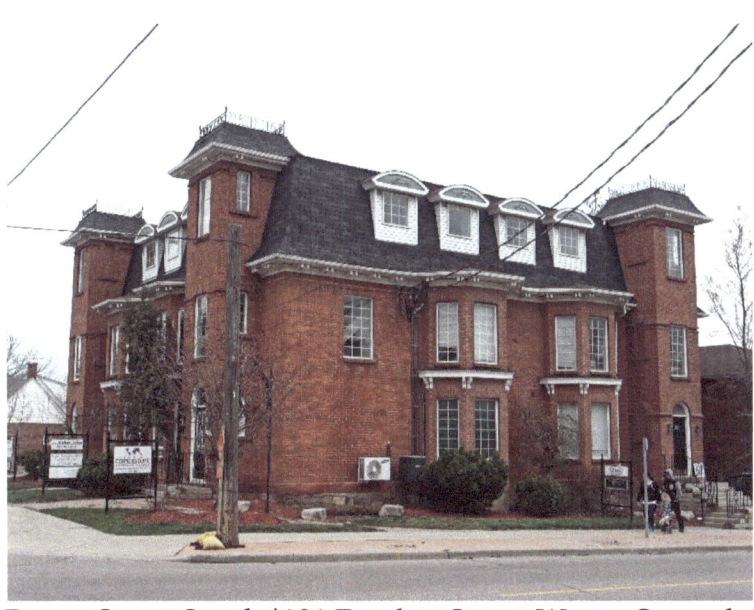

213 Byron Street South/101 Dunlop Street West – Second
Empire style, mansard roof with dormers, corner towers with
widow walks, two-storey bay windows

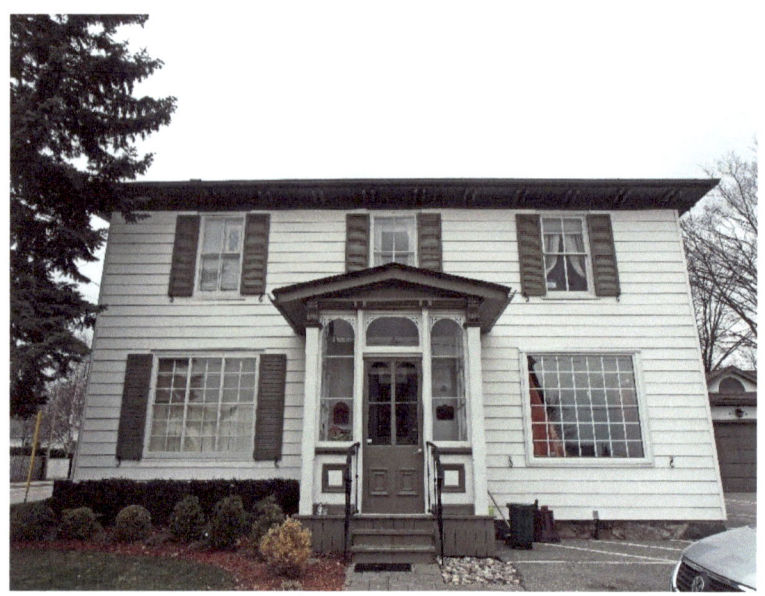

208 Byron Street South – built in 1868 – All Saints Rectory from 1882 to 1951 – tongue-in-groove frame house

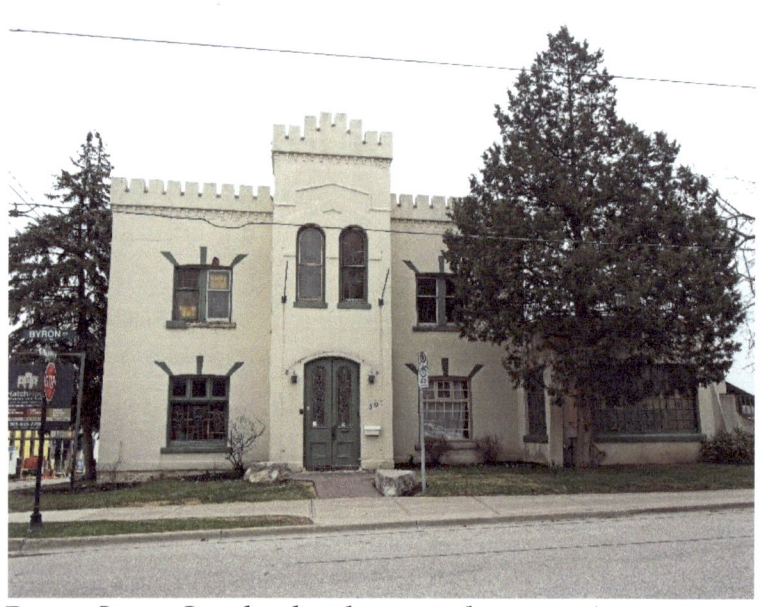

301 Byron Street South – battlemented parapet, two-storey frontispiece

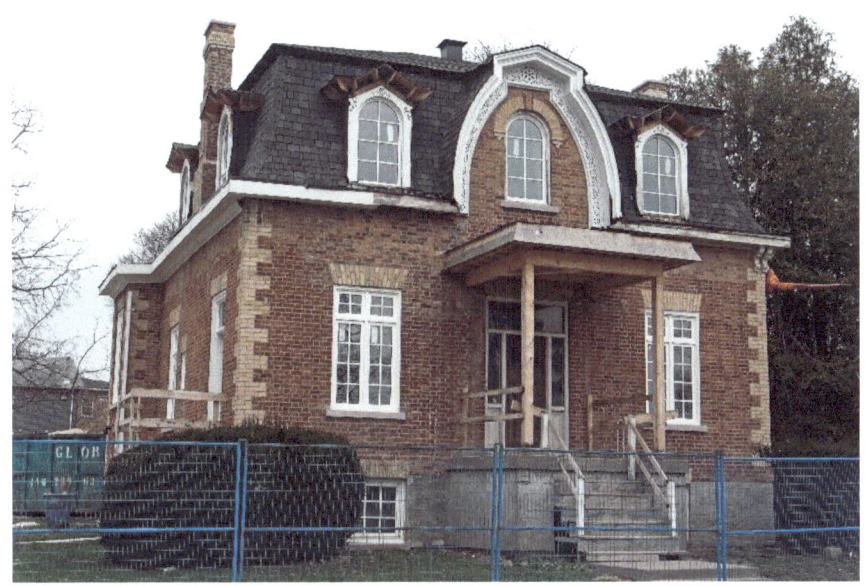

408 Byron Street South – c. 1853 – Holmes/Whitfield House - Second Empire style with mansard roof added about 1875

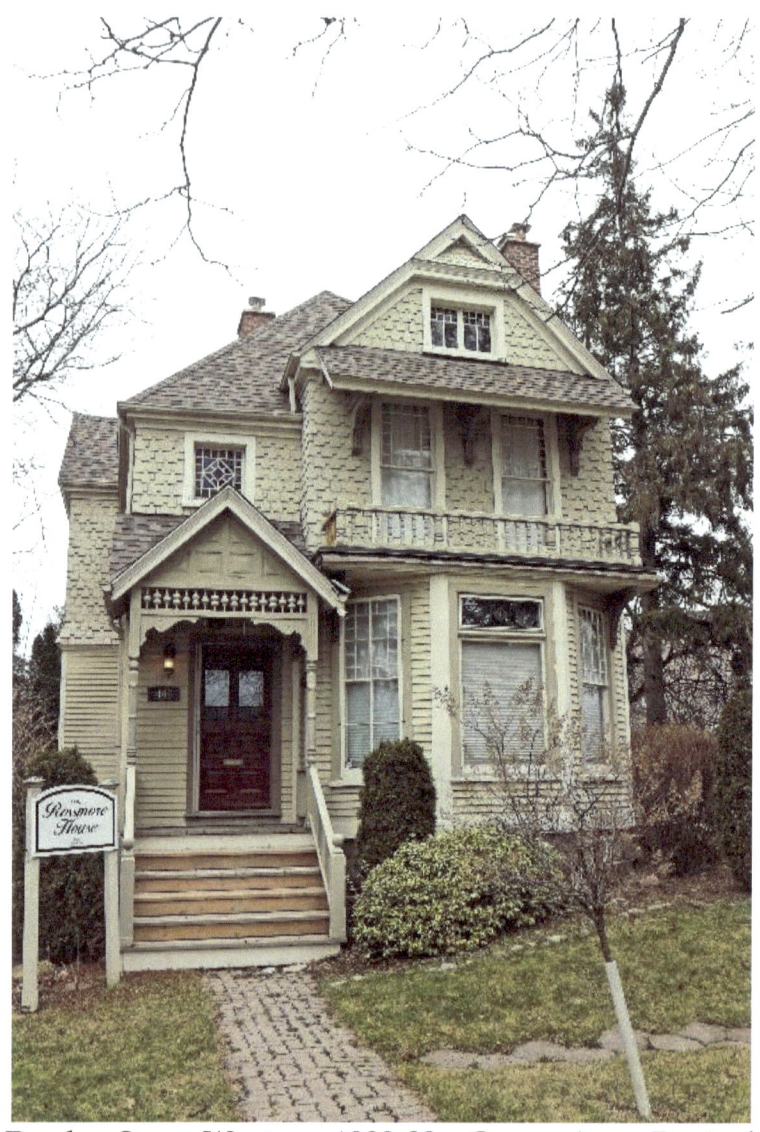

404 Dunlop Street West – c. 1888-89 – Queen Anne Revival style – asymmetrical design – built for George Ross – Mrs. Ross was president of Whitby Women's Institute and founder of the Victorian Order of Nurses in Ontario County.

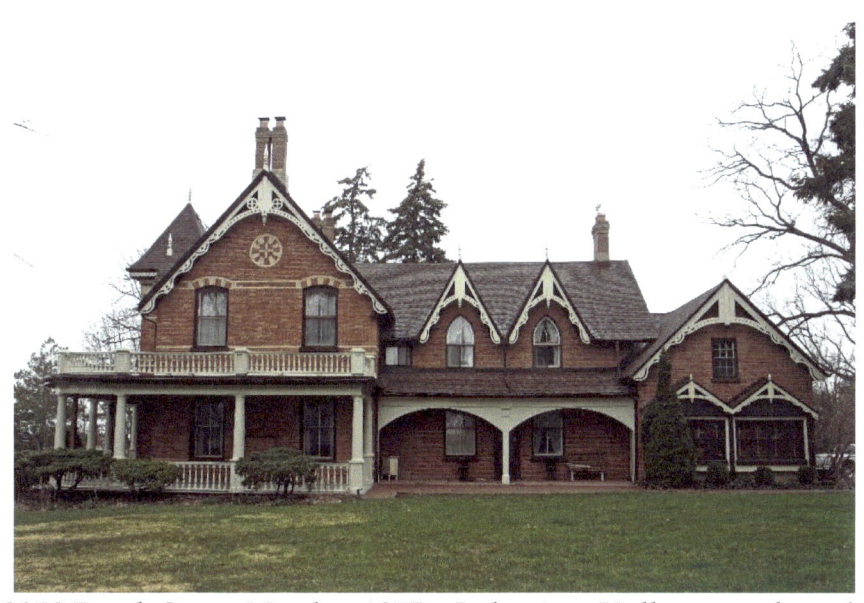

3050 Brock Street North – 1875 – Lakeview Hall – verge board trim on gables with finials, dichromatic brickwork, banding, voussoirs, two-storey wraparound veranda

Whitby, Ontario – Book 2 - in Colour Photos – My Top 14 Picks

First Nations people were the original inhabitants of the area that would become Brooklin. In the 1820s European pioneers established a small settlement in the area. The settlement expanded in the 1840s when brothers John and Robert Campbell established a flour mill on Lynde Creek. Most of the buildings in the area of the walking tour are single-detached houses. It is a diverse collection of traditional architectural styles from the mid-nineteenth to mid-twentieth centuries. These diverse styles complement the landscape as the spaces between buildings offer glimpses of the creek, small parks, and treed open spaces.

In 1819, John Scadding, clerk for Lieutenant-Governor John Graves Simcoe, was awarded a large tract of land now known as Port Whitby. Originally known as Port Windsor, the area encompassed the natural harbour in the south up to Victoria Street in the north. Soon after settlement, the harbour was used to ship local grain, lumber, and farm produce across Canada and the United States. Farmers transported their produce to Port Windsor using a plank toll road, now Brock Street, and the Port Whitby, Port Perry, and Lindsay Railway. From the 1840s to the 1870s, Windsor Harbour prospered, leading to a number of developments that modernized the harbour's infrastructure and surrounding industry. It was also during this time, in 1847, that Windsor Harbour was officially renamed Whitby Harbour. The bustling community of Port Whitby sprung up around the harbour with a number of houses, hotels, shops, and breweries supporting further development. Port Whitby, including the harbour, was one of three communities that formed the original Town of Whitby in 1855 along with Hamer's Corners and Perry's Corners.

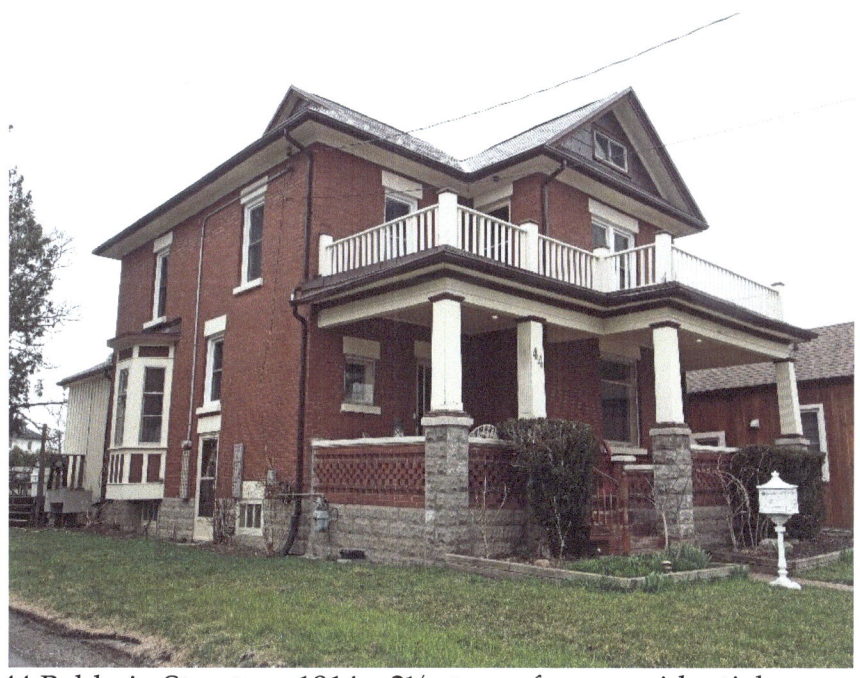

44 Baldwin Street - c. 1914 – 2½ storey frame residential building in the Edwardian Classic style, brick cladding, hip gable roof, L-shape with a wing projecting from the main block gable end to the street, a flat-roofed verandah with open porch above

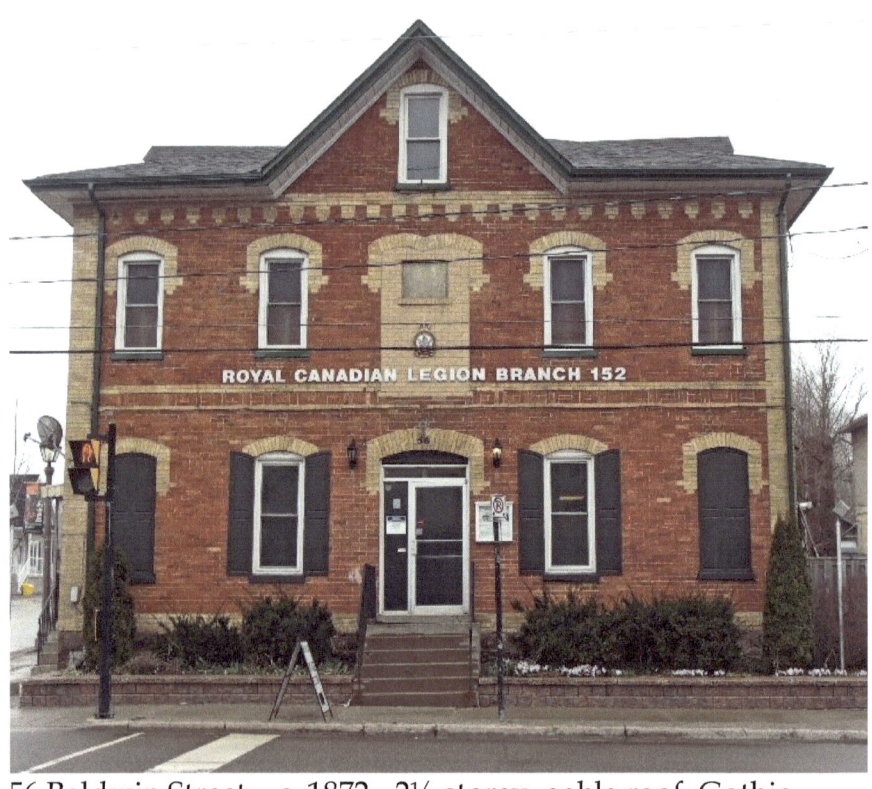

56 Baldwin Street – c. 1872 - 2½ storey, gable roof, Gothic Revival influences, decorative brick drip mouldings over windows, decorative brick band courses, foundation and pilasters at corners – Royal Canadian Legion

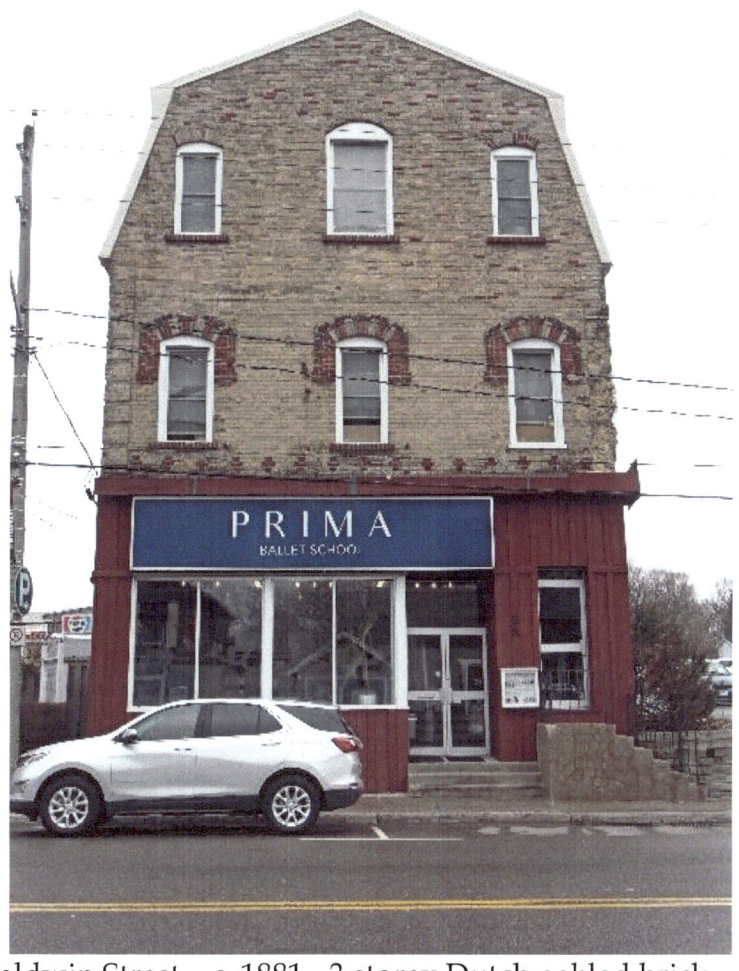

58 Baldwin Street – c. 1881 - 3 storey Dutch gabled brick
commercial building with Gothic Revival influences,
decorative brick drip mouldings on second storey windows,
decorative brick sills, decorative brick medallions over first
storey signboard

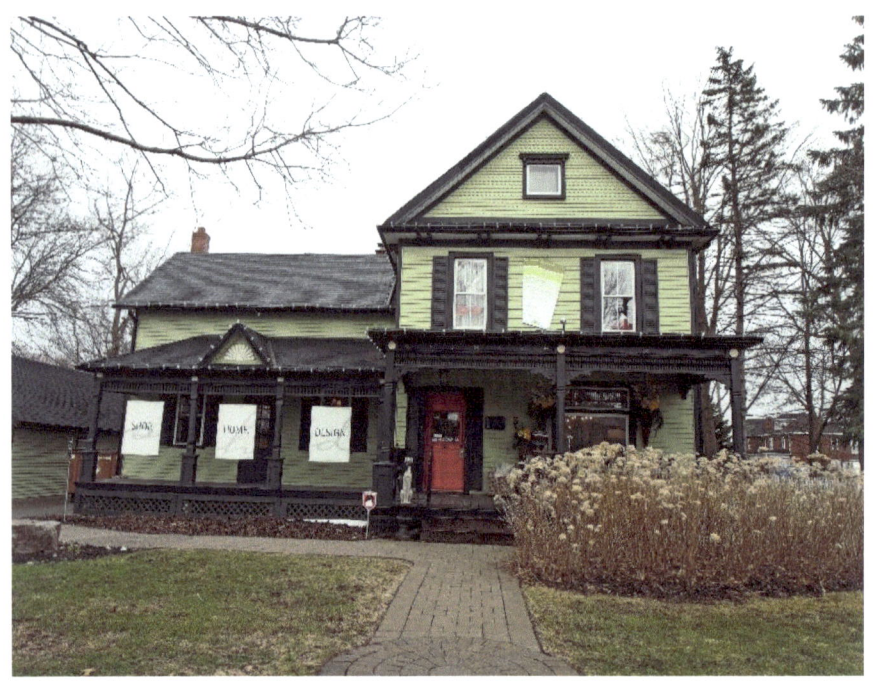

3 Cassels Road East – c. 1889 – 2½ storey frame gable roofed Victorian vernacular home was built by Charles Grass and owned by the Grass family until 1950. For many years he operated, but did not own the mill. The main block has the gable end to street, with a 1½ storey wing to the east and a projecting gable roofed bay to the west, clapboard siding, fish scale siding on gable end, decorative cornice and brackets on verandah, stained glass over first storey window.

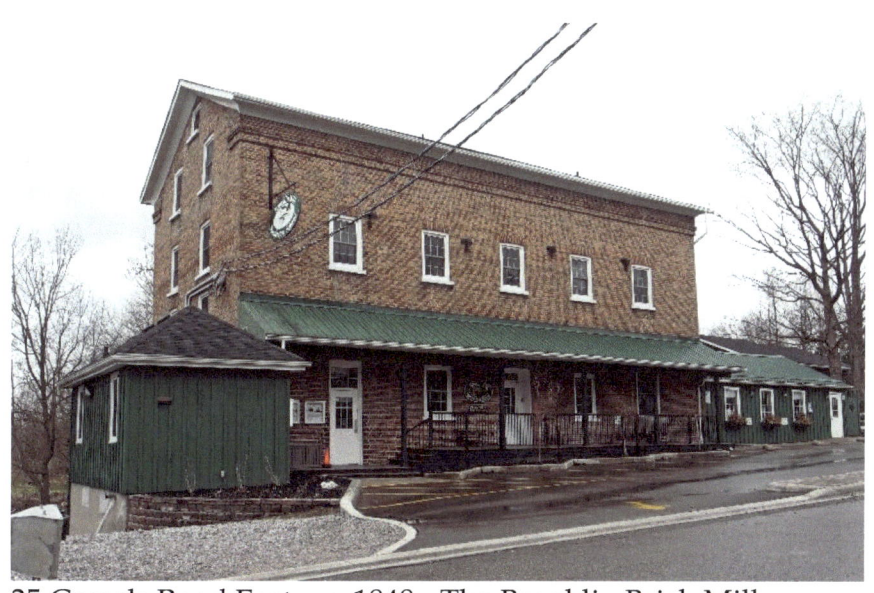

25 Cassels Road East – c. 1848 - The Brooklin Brick Mill was
built for John Campbell after the original frame mill (1840)
was destroyed by fire. The cedar swamp that originally
covered the site was filled so that the foundation could be
built on solid ground. The date is still visible on the west side
gable. The mill could produce 50 barrels of flour a day and
operated as a flour mill for 149 years, ceasing operation in
1991.

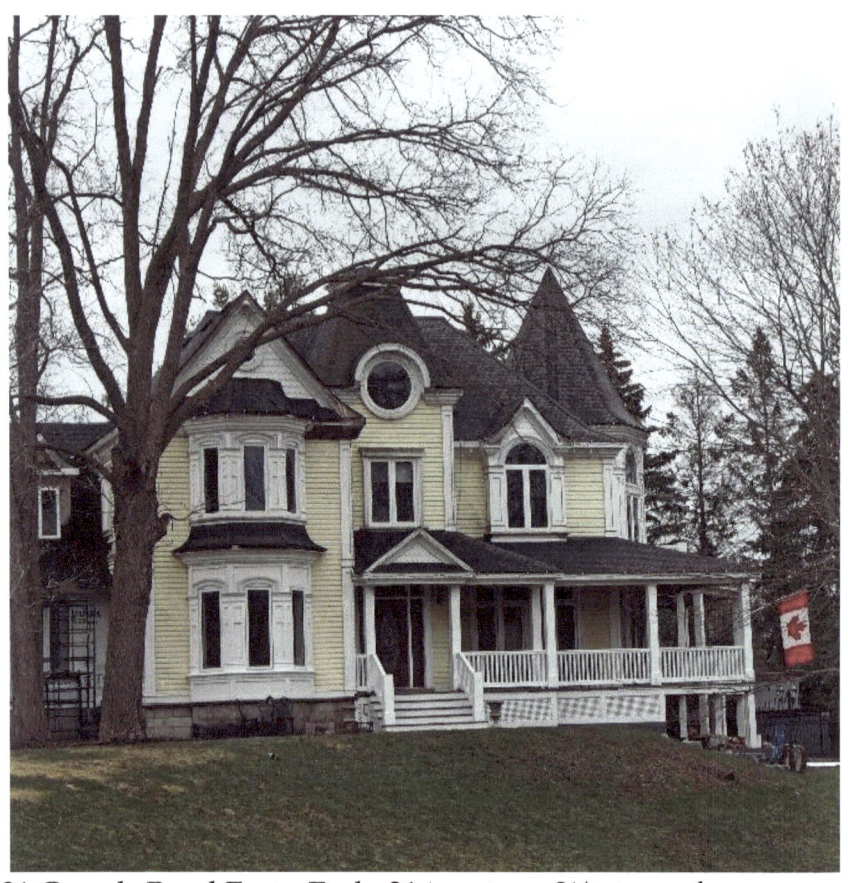

31 Cassels Road East - Early 21st century 2½ storey frame complex gable roofed residential building with eclectic late 19th century stylistic influences (mansarded central bay, turreted and gabled side bays, projecting bay windows, Palladian windows

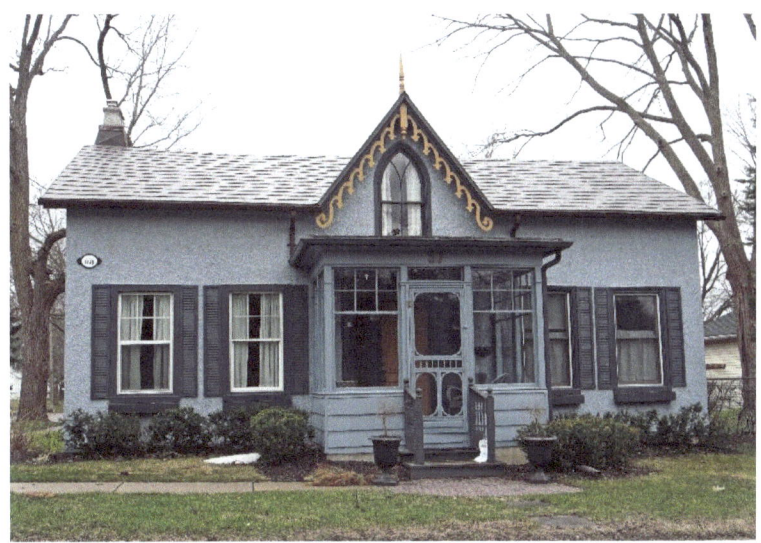

57 Cassels Road East – c. 1848 - Gothic Revival style, central entranceway within a flat roofed enclosed porch, Gothic-arched window above, decorative barge board and finial

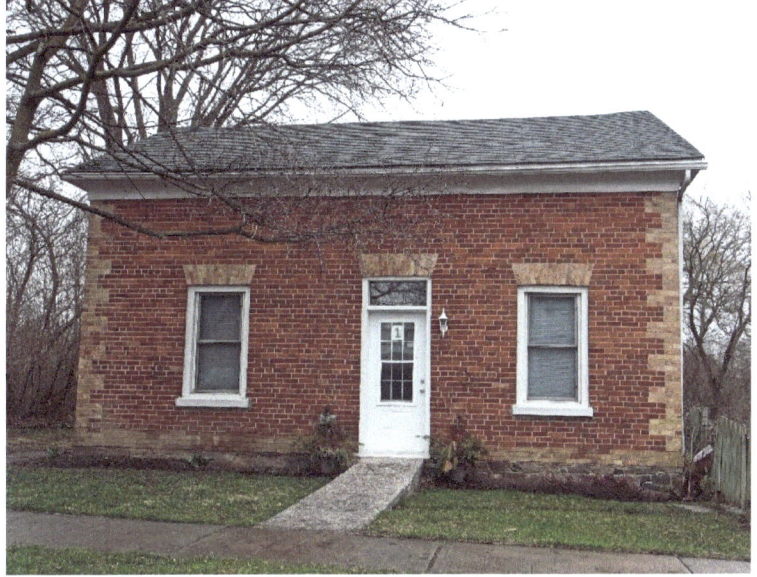

1 Princess Street – c. 1857 - 1½ storey brick gable roofed residential building, with a slightly offset central entranceway flanked by two windows, buff brick cornices on windows and door and quoins

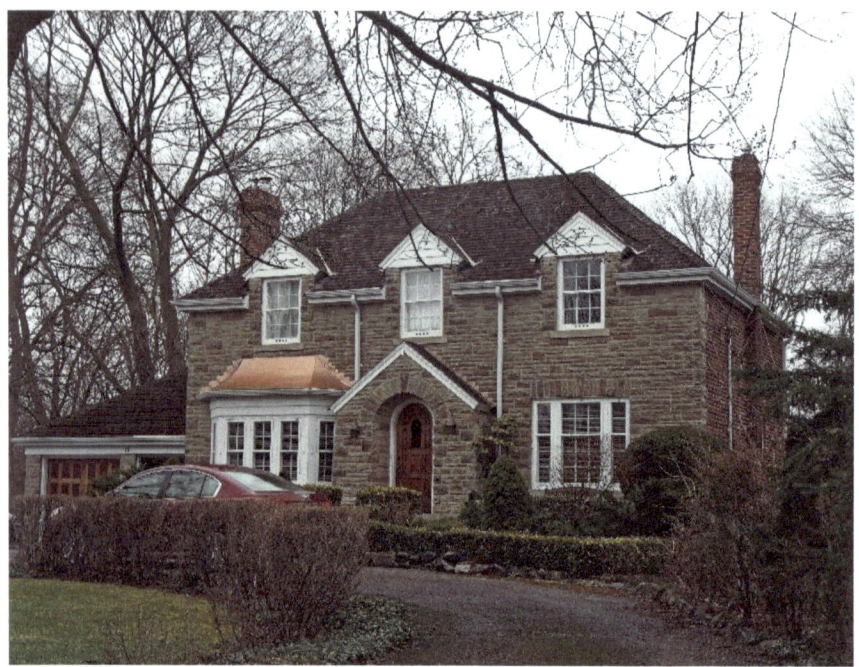

11 Princess Street – c. 1943 - stone and brick hip gable roofed house - It has a tapestry brickwork pattern with an ashlar stone pattern (square cut building stones) on the street façade. Arthur James Cook, a Township Councillor in 1933/34, built the house after retiring from his business as a butcher shop owner.

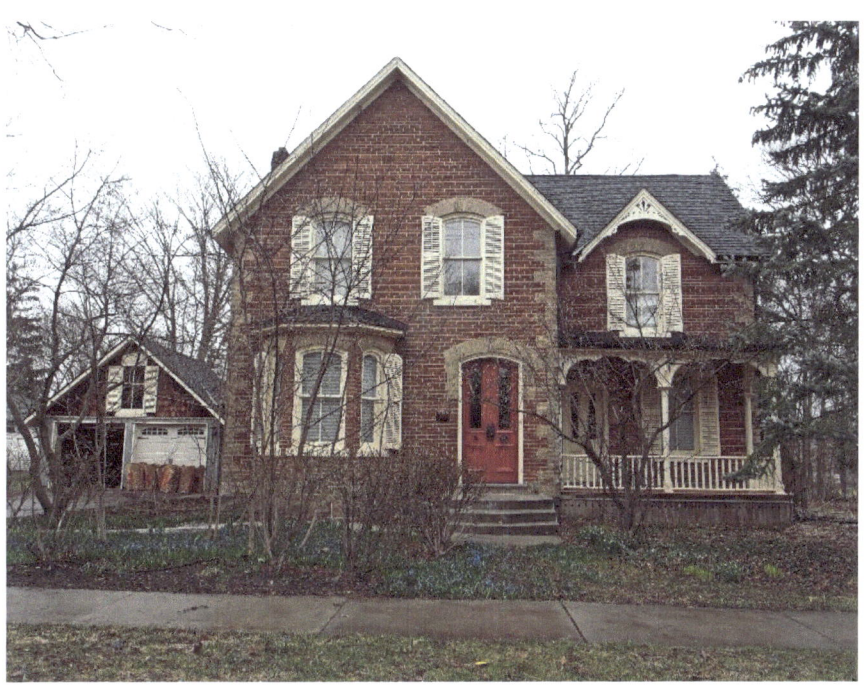

15 Princess Street – Benjamin Franklin Campbell House – c. 1877 - Gothic Revival style, large gable end block with a recessed block to the south, bay window, 2-over-2 curved top windows, ornamental white brick lintels and quoins, wooden shutters, panelled wood and glass main and secondary doors, decorative barge boarding on the porch and roof gable

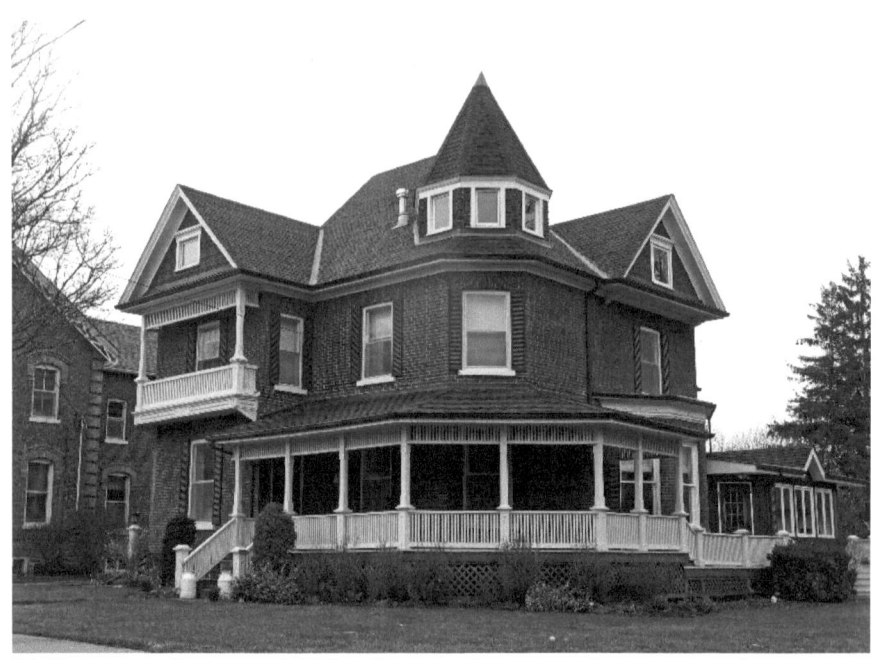

21 Princess Street – 1895 - Queen Anne style, engaged tower, chevron pattern shingles on west gable and basket weave pattern on the tower, balcony and verandah wooden railings

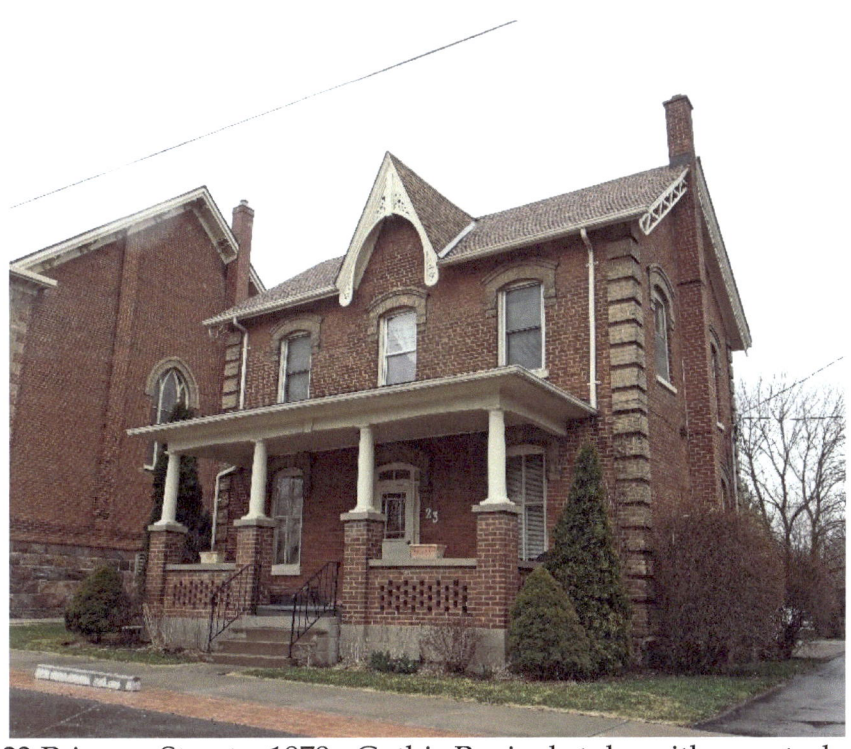

23 Princess Street – 1879 - Gothic Revival style, with a central entrance panelled wooden door with top light contained in a round-headed panelled wooden door surround with decorative brick lintel/drip moulding, flanked by two 2/2 elongated windows with similar lintels, under a shed roofed full width porch supported by turned wooden posts on brick plinths, with three similar windows in the second storey above, with the central window centred under a roof gable. It was built as a Methodist parsonage by A.P. Cameron; it cost $1,700 to construct. In 1917, it became one of the first buildings to be wired for electricity in Brooklin.

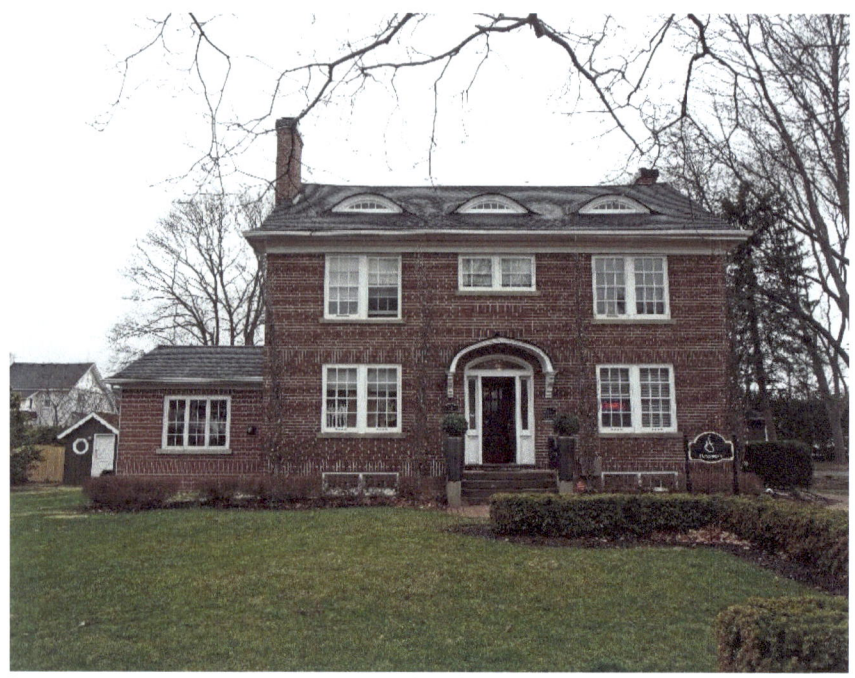

24 Princess Street – c. 1935 – This house was built by Dr. John Moore who came to Brooklin in 1891 and was a doctor here for 46 years. He was Reeve of Whitby Township from 1912-14 and served on the Brooklin School Board. The English cross bond brick pattern is rare to see and would have been expensive to produce. Central entranceway with glazed top and side lights under a slightly projecting bracketed curving wooden lintel, flanked by 6/6 double windows in the first and second storeys, with a 3/3 double window above, three eyebrow dormers with shallow windows.

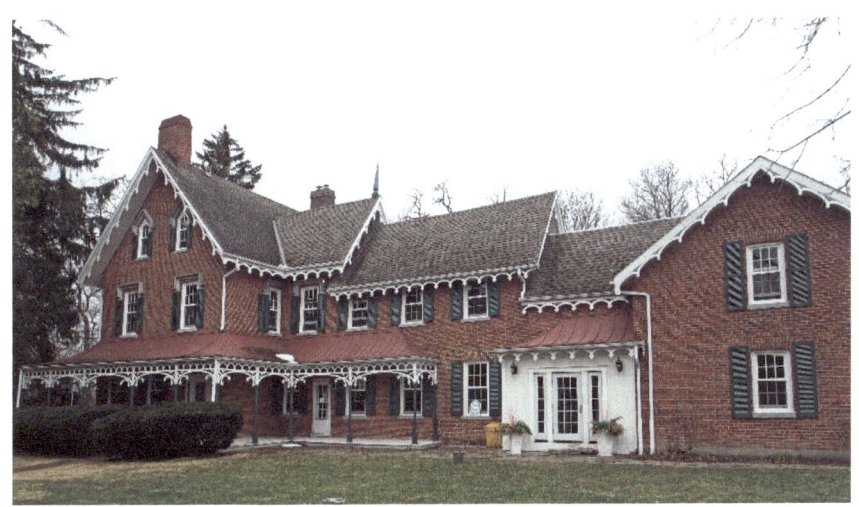

90 Colston Avenue – Stephen Thomas House – c. 1858 – 2½ storey brick gable roofed building with Gothic Revival influences - best surviving mansion and grounds from the early days of the village

Ajax and Pickering, Ontario in Colour Photos – My Top 11 Picks

Ajax is a town in Durham Region in Southern Ontario, Canada, located in the eastern part of the Greater Toronto Area. The town is named for HMS Ajax, a Royal Navy cruiser that served in World War II. It is about twenty-five kilometers (16 miles) east of Toronto on the shores of Lake Ontario and is bordered by the City of Pickering to the west and north, and the Town of Whitby to the east.

Before the Second World War, Ajax was a rural part of the township of Pickering. The town was established in 1941 when a Defense Industries Limited (D.I.L.) shell plant was constructed and a town site grew around the plant. By 1945 the plant employed over 9,000 people at peak production. It had its own water and sewage treatment plants and fifty kilometers (31 miles) of railroad and 50 kilometers (31 miles) of roads. The entire D.I.L. plant site was about twelve square kilometers (5 square miles).

Pickering is a city located in Southern Ontario, east of Toronto in Durham Region. It was settled by British colonists starting in the 1770s. Many of the smaller rural communities have been preserved and function as provincially significant historic sites and museums.

Whitevale, formerly Majorville, is a community located within the City of Pickering. The community was first settled in the 1820s when John Major built a sawmill; there were many Majors living in the area. Around 1855 Truman P. White bought the saw mill, built a gristmill and a cooperage, and in 1866 built a planing factory. In 1867 he built a large four storey brick woolen mill. The community owed so much of its development and business prosperity to T.P. White that in acknowledgement, it adopted Whitevale as its permanent name. In 1855, Donald McPhee opened the first store.

In 1890 Whitevale contained a stave and heading factory and a barrel factory both owned and operated by the Spink brothers; three general stores, one owned by James Taylor and Donald McPhee; a wagon and carriage factory, operated by the Pollard brothers; a cheese factory, owned and operated by P.R. Hoover and Company; the merchant and tailoring firm of J. Rose and Son; the shoemaker shops of John Allen and D. Moodey; the butcher shop of Israel Burton and the tinsmith shop of S.B. Wigmore. In addition, Whitevale contained two blacksmiths, two wagon shops, a school house, undertakers, harness shop, grist mill, brush factory, grindstone factory, barber shop, three dressmakers, three gardeners, money order and post offices, hotel, brass band, two churches and four lodges.

The Whitevale Heritage Conservation District was established to ensure the preservation and enhancement of the special character of Whitevale. It is dominated by its rural setting and modest vernacular buildings; the hamlet has not changed significantly in character since the late 19th century. The building style in Whitevale is a mixture of typical rural Ontario vernacular architecture combined with Victorian influences and materials in common usage at the time of construction. The overall nineteenth century village character has been retained.

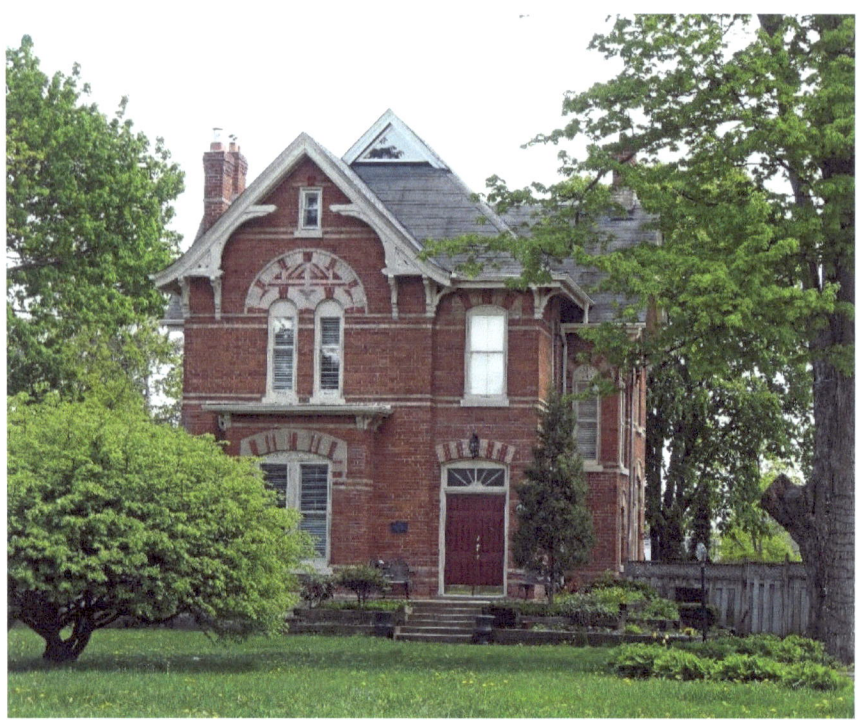

497 Kingston Road West, Historic Pickering Village (now in Ajax) – 1870 - purchased in 1882 by Dr. Field for his daughter. Dr. Field was a practicing physician in Pickering Village and later built his own home directly east of this property. In 1929, Emerson & Henrietta Bertrand purchased the home and raised Allan Irwin. The family gave up the homestead in 1934, only to have it reclaimed in 1977 by their grandson, B. B. Bertrand (son of Allan). The building is a 2½ storey brick structure in Italianate architecture.

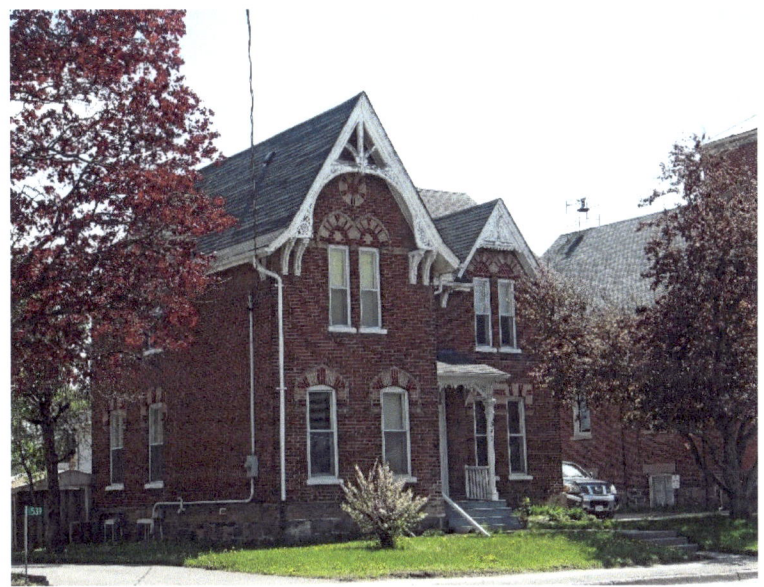

543 Kingston Road West, Historic Pickering Village (now in Ajax) – dichromatic voussoirs

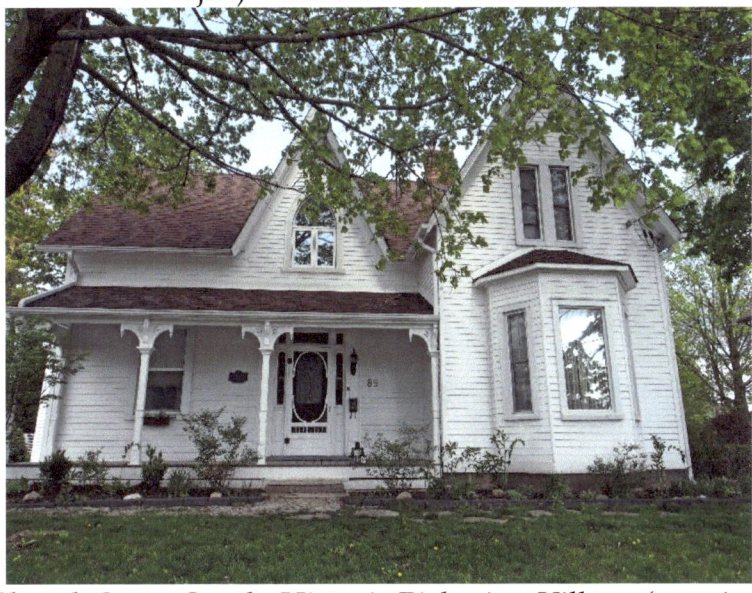

89 Church Street South, Historic Pickering Village (now in Ajax) - This home, built in 1877, has existed in its present configuration since 1937. It is the best-preserved frame house of Gothic Revival design within the Town of Ajax.

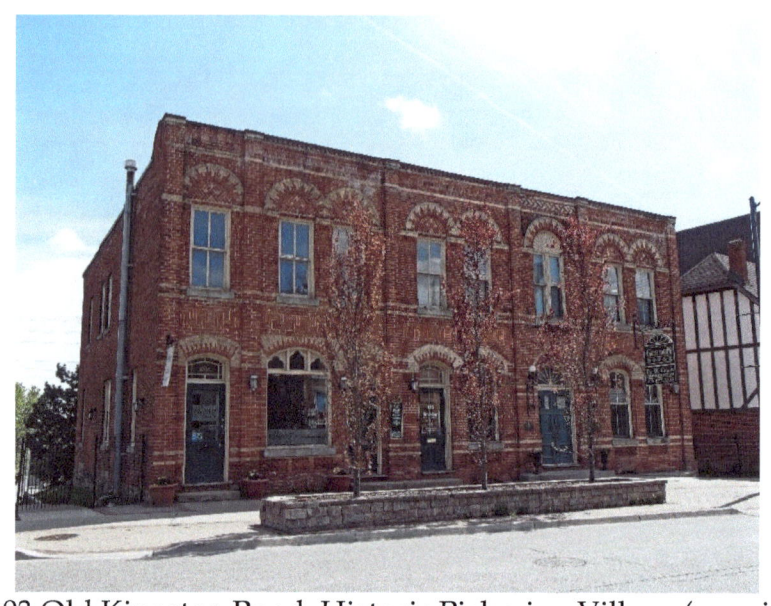

103 Old Kingston Road, Historic Pickering Village (now in Ajax) – dichromatic voussoirs

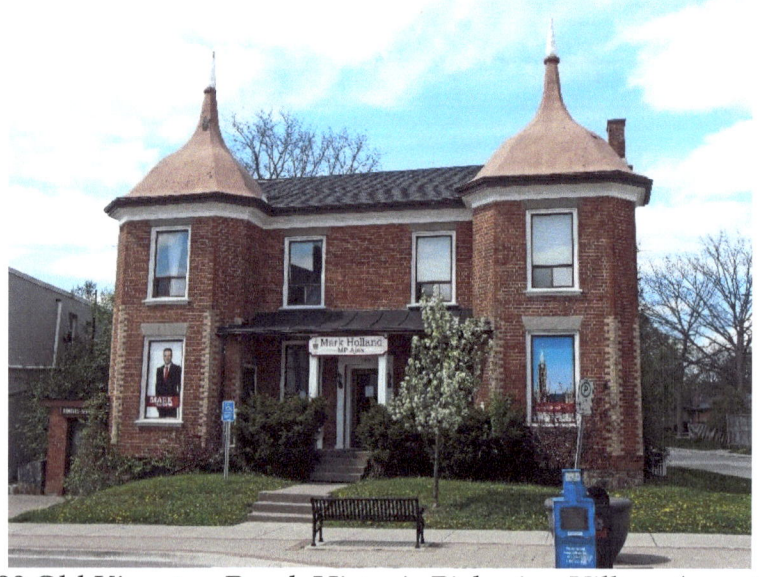

100 Old Kingston Road, Historic Pickering Village (now in Ajax) - twin two-storey capped towers

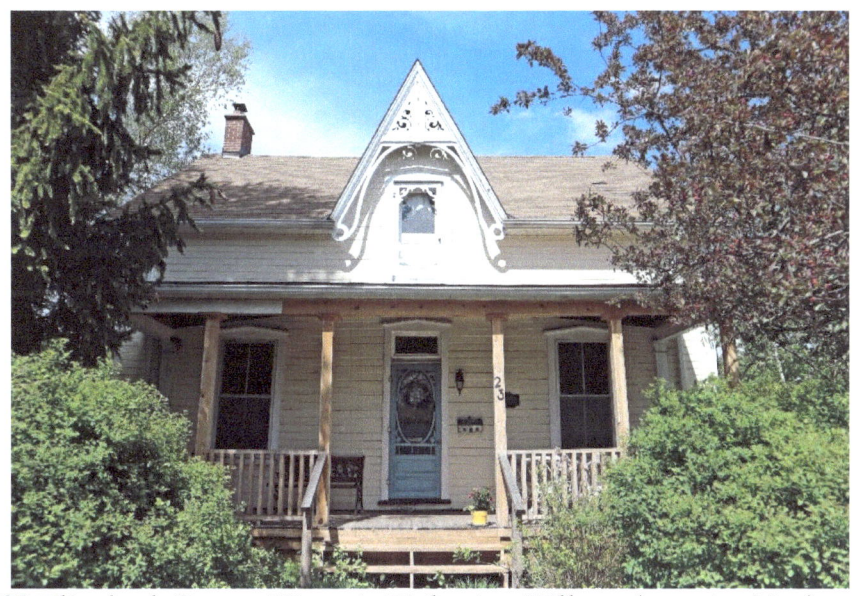

23 Elizabeth Street, Historic Pickering Village (now in Ajax) - This Gothic house was built in 1875. In 1980 the owners restored the tongue and grove pine wood facade. Other features include the decorative trim above the front gable and a second storey "suicide" door. Tradition says is was the first house equipped with inside plumbing and central heating - features installed to persuade a retired miller from Toronto to run the Spink's Mill on nearby Duffin's Creek during World War I.

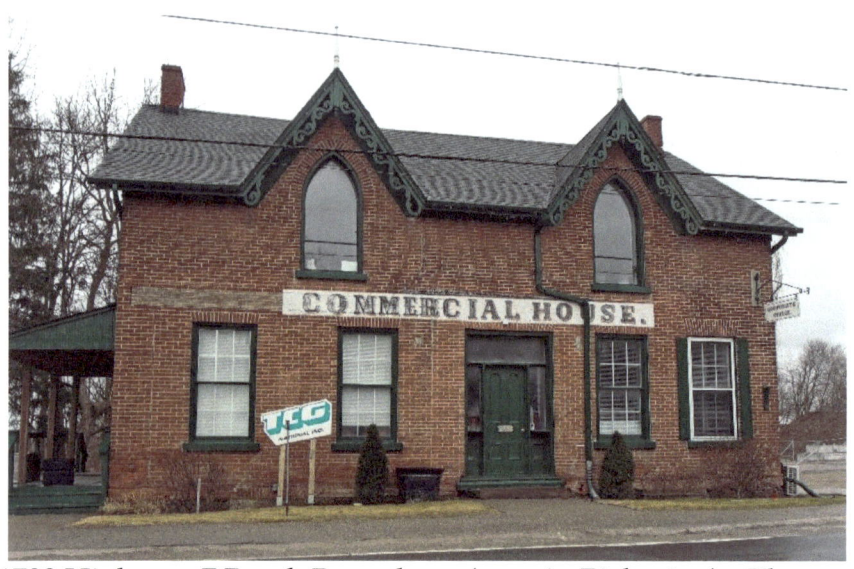

1709 Highway 7 Road, Brougham (now in Pickering) - The Former Commercial Hotel in Brougham, Ontario is a two-storey brick building in the Gothic Revival style with a gable roof and has pointed arched windows in two dormers with finials and decorative wood fascia. It was initially built as a home and then converted into a hotel.

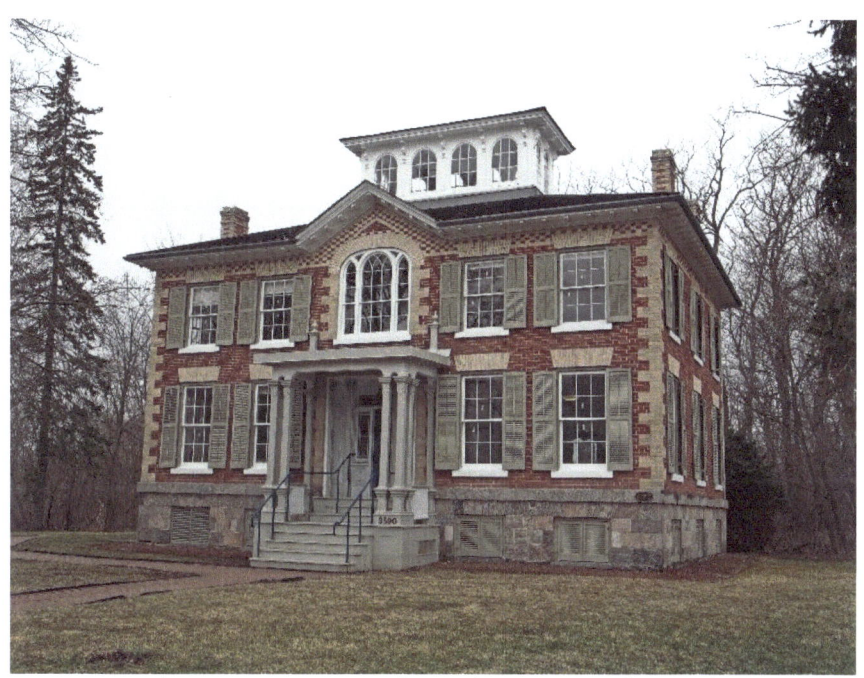

Bentley House, Brougham (now in Pickering) - was built in 1853-55 for William Bentley, a local businessman and founder of Brougham village. It remained in the Bentley family until 1959, when it was purchased and restored by the Gibson family. The site is now part of the proposed Pickering Airport. Bentley House, on its original four-acre site, is located at the intersection of the Brock Road and Highway 7.

The Italianate style has two variations. The Tuscan Villa style reflects the Picturesque values of variety in silhouette and textures and intricacy in detail, while the Italian Palazzo form emphasizes the symmetry and tripartite composition typical of Renaissance buildings. The heritage character of Bentley House resides in its vernacular Italianate style, as evidenced by the combination of Renaissance massing with Picturesque expression in the materials and detailing.

The Renaissance influence on the design of Bentley House is reflected in its symmetrical massing, shallow hip roof, regular arrangement of windows on all façades, and round-headed windows in the belvedere. Picturesque qualities are expressed in the variety of colors and textures of materials: stone foundation, polychrome red-and-buff brickwork, large multi-paned sash windows, and elaborate wood trim and wood belvedere. The emphasis on ornamentation typical of Italianate villas in the Picturesque tradition is reflected in the tracery of the segmentally-arched window in the gable, eave brackets and dentils on both the house and belvedere, paneled door casing with carved colonnettes in antis, carved porch pillars, window shutters, and prominent decorative chimneys.

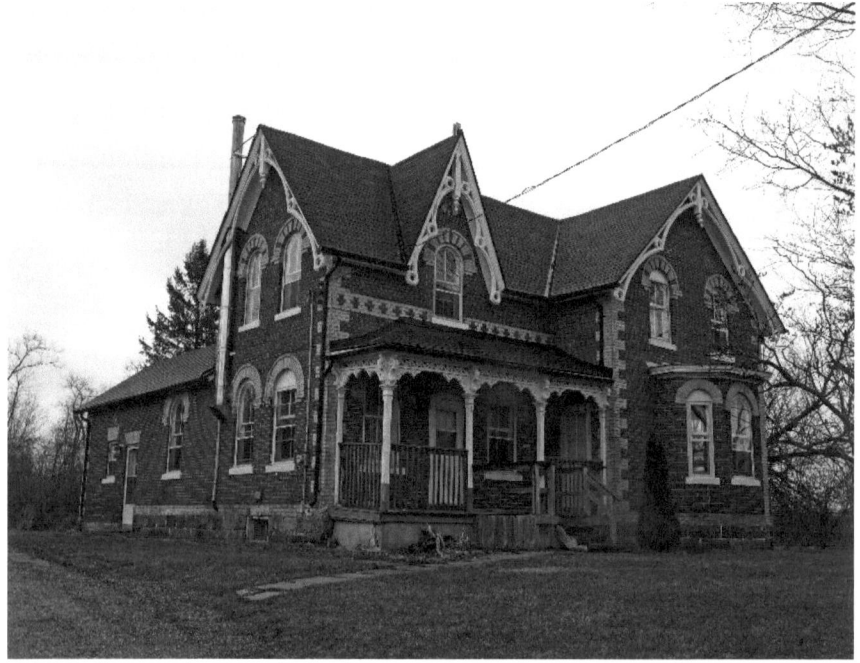

1200 Whitevale Road, Pickering – Gothic – verge board trim and finials on gables, banding, corner quoins, bay window

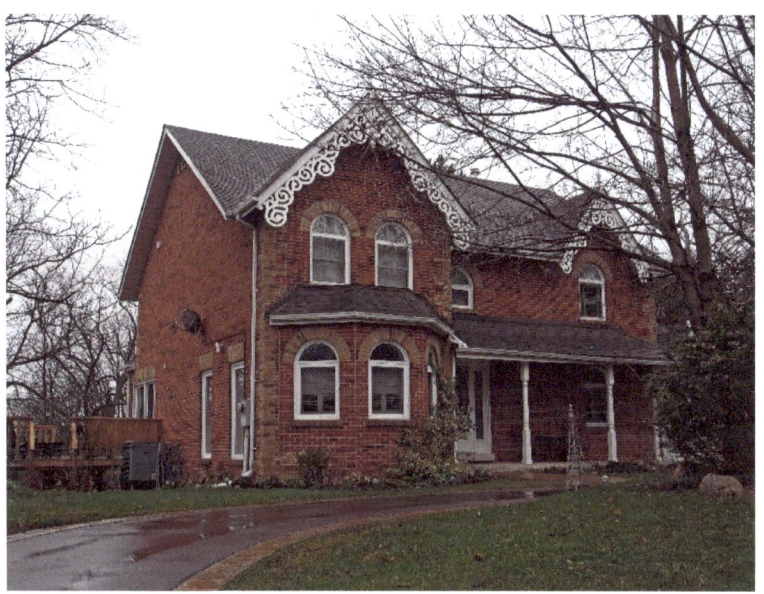

Whitevale (now in Pickering) - Golf Club Road

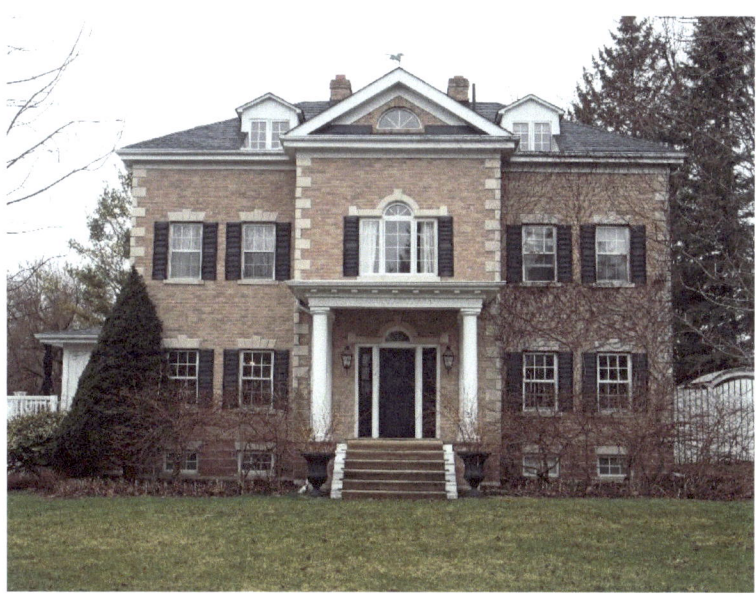

Whitevale - 3180 Byron Street – two-storey frontispiece with fanlight in gable pediment, corner quoins, dormers, voussoirs with keystones, shutters, sidelights and fanlight about door and matching French window above porch

Oshawa, Ontario – Book 1 - in Colour Photos – My Top 4 Picks

Oshawa is a city in Southern Ontario on the Lake Ontario shoreline. It is about sixty kilometres east of Downtown Toronto. The name Oshawa comes from the Ojibwa word meaning "the crossing place" or "where we must leave our canoes". More than 5,000 people work and more than 2,400 university students study in the downtown core.

Oshawa's roots are tied to the automobile industry with the Canadian division of General Motors located here. It was founded in 1876 as the McLaughlin Carriage Company. The lavish home of the carriage company's founder, Parkwood Estate, is a National Historic Site of Canada.

Historians believe that Oshawa began as a transfer point for the fur trade. Beaver and other animals trapped for their pelts by local natives were traded with the Coureurs des bois (voyagers). Furs were loaded onto canoes by the Mississauga Indians at the Oshawa harbor and transported to the trading posts located to the west at the mouth of the Credit River. Around 1760, the French constructed a trading post near the harbor location; this was abandoned after a few years, but its ruins provided shelter for the first residents of what later became Oshawa.

In the late eighteenth century, a local resident, Roger Conant, started an export business shipping salmon to the United States. His success attracted further migration into the region. A large number of the founding immigrants were United Empire Loyalists, who left the United States to live under British rule. Later Irish and then French-Canadian immigration increased as did industrialization. Oshawa and the surrounding Ontario County were the settling grounds of a large number of nineteenth century Cornish immigrants.

The surveys ordered by Governor John Graves Simcoe, and subsequent land grants, helped populate the area. When Col. Asa Danforth laid out his York-to-Kingston road, it passed through the Oshawa area. In 1822, a "colonization road" (a north-south road to facilitate settlement) known as Simcoe Street was constructed. It ran from the harbor to the area of Lake Scugog. It intersected the "Kingston Road: at what became Oshawa's "Four Corners."

In 1846 there were about 1,000 people in a community surrounded by farms. There were three churches, a post office, and tradesmen of various types, a foundry, a grist mill and a fulling mill, a brewery, two distilleries, a machine shop and four cabinet makers.

The village became an industrial center, and implement works, tanneries, asheries and wagon factories opened. In 1876, Robert Samuel McLaughlin, Sr. moved his carriage works to Oshawa from Enniskillen to take advantage of its harbor and of the availability of a rail link not too far away. He constructed a two-storey building, which was soon added to. This building was heavily remodeled in 1929, receiving a new facade and being extended to the north. Around 1890, the carriage works relocated from its Simcoe Street address to an unused furniture factory a couple of blocks to the northeast, and this remained its site until the building burnt in 1899. Offered assistance by the town, McLaughlin chose to stay in Oshawa, building a new factory across Mary Street from the old site. Rail service had been provided in 1890 by the Oshawa Railway; this was originally set up as a streetcar line, but by about 1910 a second freight line was built slightly to the east of Simcoe Street which provided streetcar and freight service, connected central Oshawa with the Grand Trunk (now Canadian National) Railway, and with the Canadian Northern (which ran through the very north of Oshawa) and the Canadian Pacific, built in 1912-13.

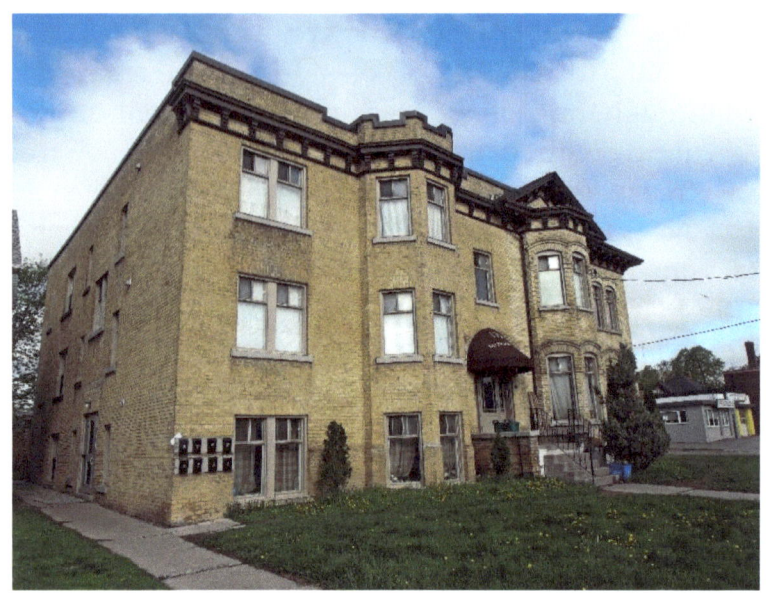

170 Simcoe Street South – 1925 – battlementing above three-storey bay window on left

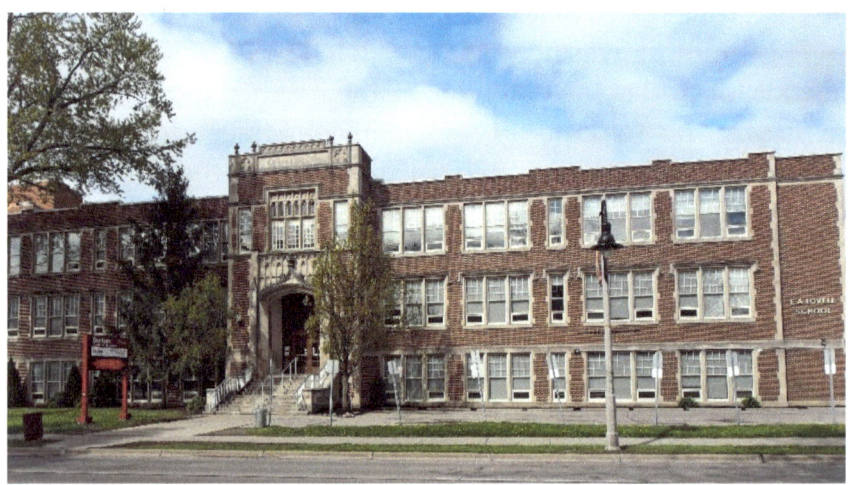

120 Centre Street South - EA Lovell School - 1924

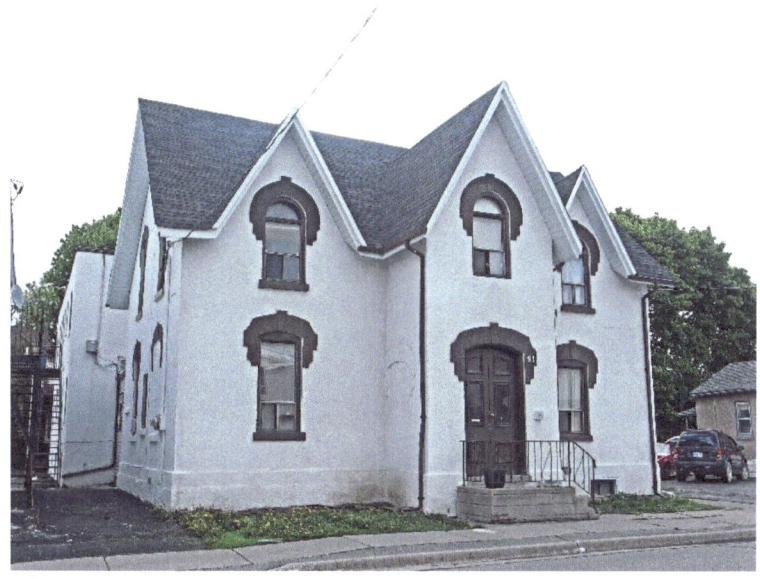

91 Celina Street – c. 1890 – Gothic style – decorative drip molds with keystones around windows and doors

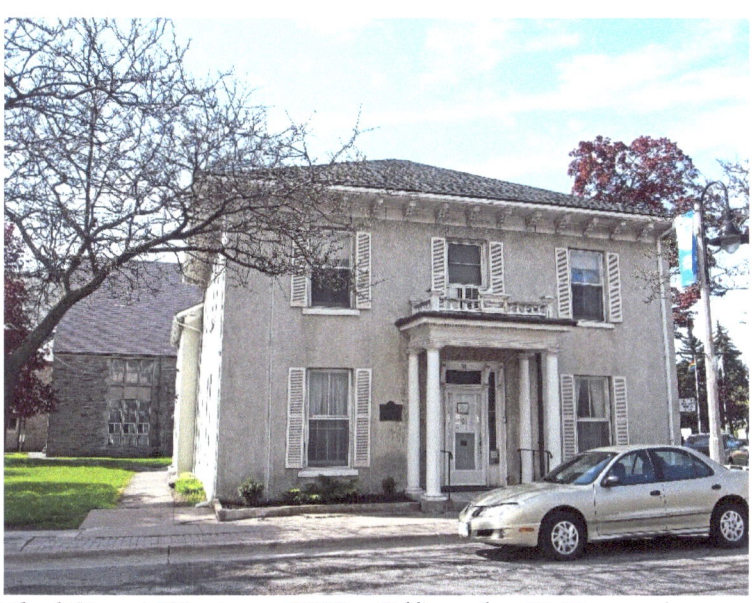

39 Athol Street West – c. 1858 - Offices for St George's Memorial Anglican Church – cornice brackets, second floor balcony above pillared entrance

Oshawa, Ontario – Book 2 - in Colour Photos – My Top 4 Picks

Oshawa is a city in Southern Ontario on the Lake Ontario shoreline. It is about sixty kilometres east of Downtown Toronto.

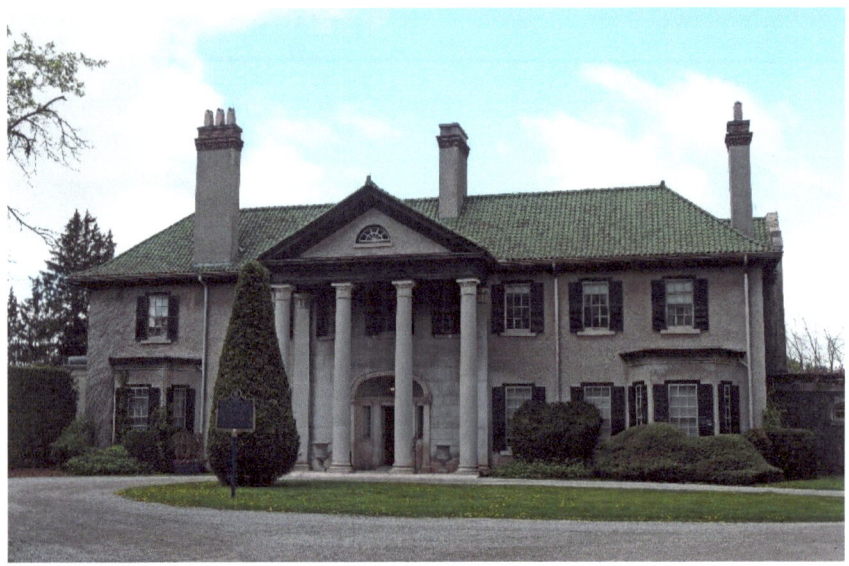

270 Simcoe Street North – Parkwood, McLaughlin Estate - Colonel Robert Samuel McLaughlin and "Billy" Durant signed a 15-year contract in 1907, under which the McLaughlin Motor Company began to manufacture automobiles under the McLaughlin name, using Buick engines and other mechanical parts. Buick was merged into General Motors shortly after, and in 1915 the firm acquired the manufacturing rights to the Chevrolet brand. Within three years, the McLaughlin Motor Car Company and the Chevrolet Motor Car Company of Canada merged, creating General Motors of Canada in 1918 with McLaughlin as President.

With the wealth he gained in his business venture, in 1916 McLaughlin built one of the stateliest homes in Canada, "Parkwood". The 55-room residence was designed by Toronto architect John M. Lyle. McLaughlin lived in the house for 55 years with his wife and they raised five daughters. The house replaced an older mansion, which was about 30 years old when it was demolished; the grounds of the earlier home had been operated as Prospect Park, and this land was acquired by the town and became its first municipal park, Alexandra Park. Parkwood today is open to the public as a National Historic Site.

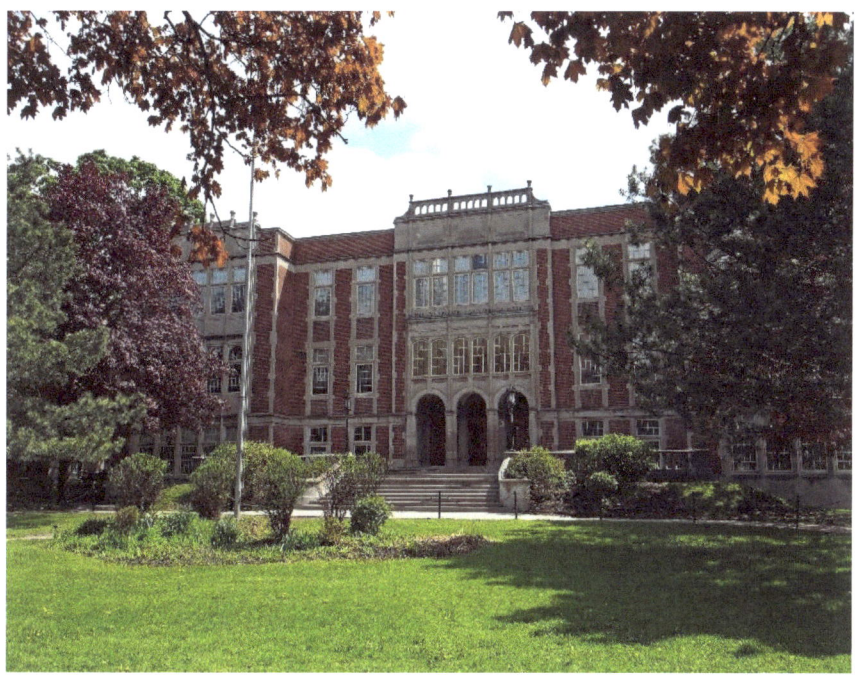

301 Simcoe Street North - O'Neill Collegiate and Vocational Institute offers a wide range of academic and extracurricular activities. It is known as an art school, drawing many students from around the Greater Toronto Area into its arts programs. The science programs are well developed, with multiple fully functional science labs.

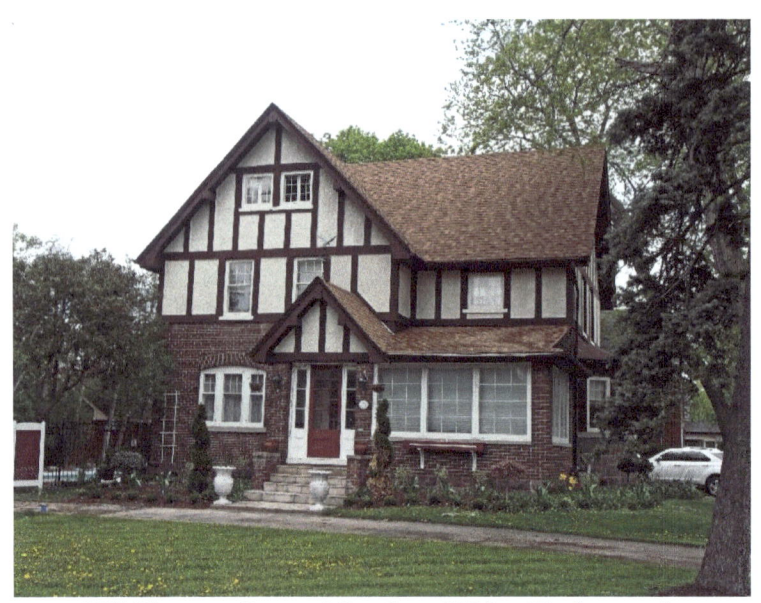

377 Simcoe Street North – 1920 – Tudor style

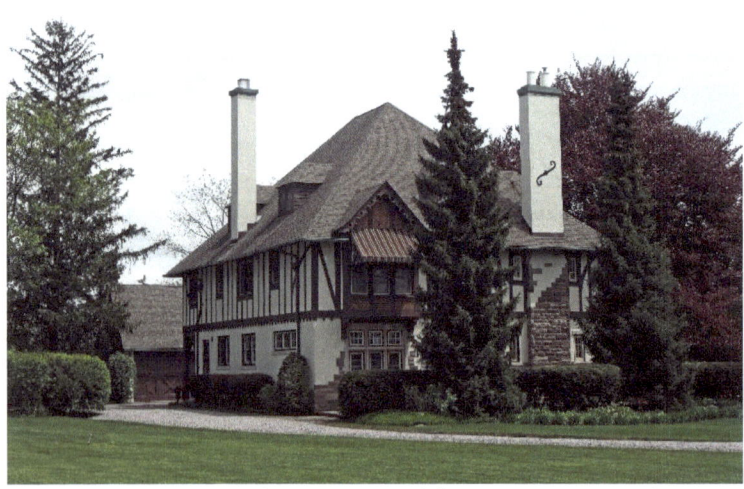

705 Simcoe Street North – McLaughlin estate Greenbriar – 1928 – Tudor style

Oshawa, Ontario – Book 3 - in Colour Photos – My Top 7 Picks

Oshawa is a city in Southern Ontario on the Lake Ontario shoreline. It is about sixty kilometres east of Downtown Toronto.

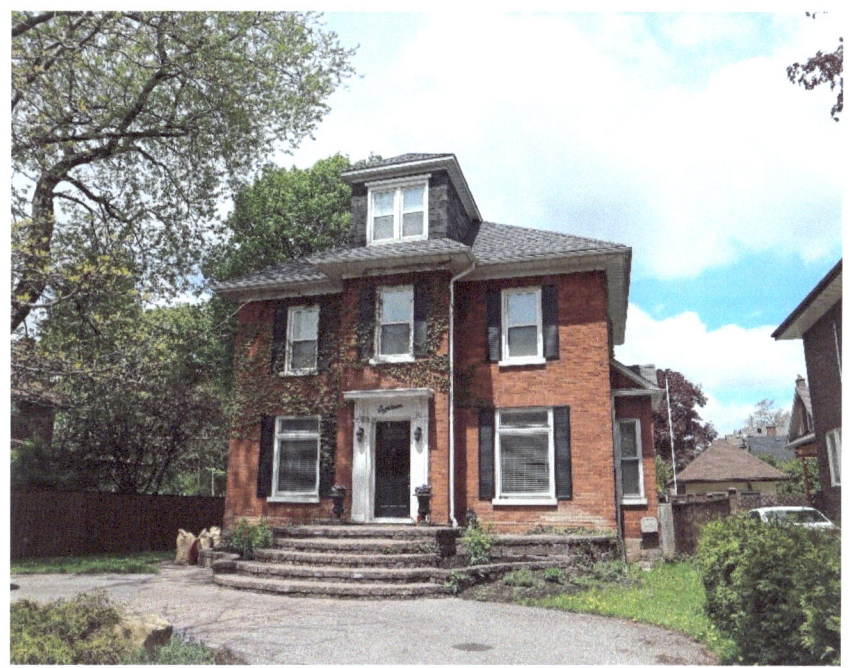

18 Aberdeen Street

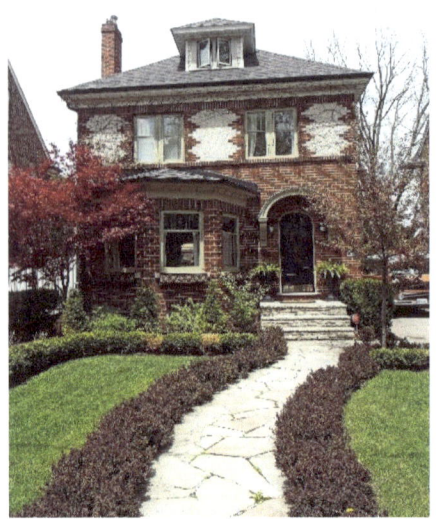

43 Connaught Street

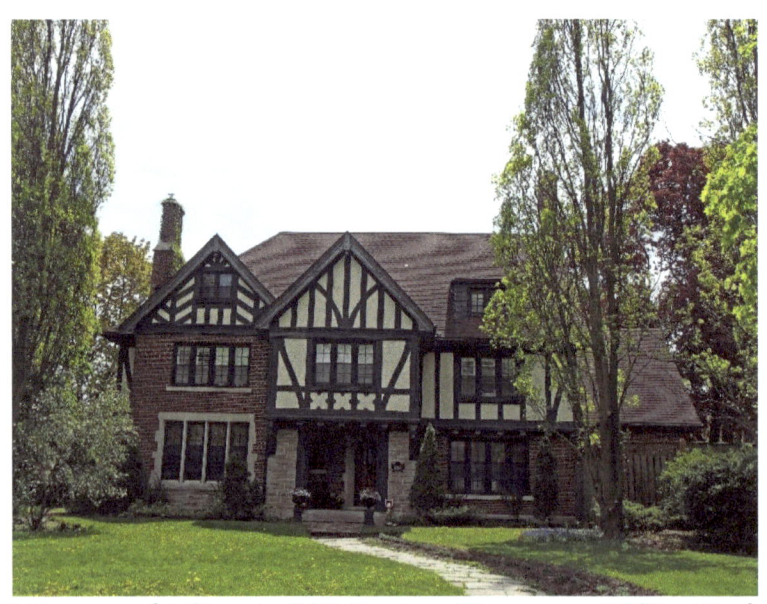

55 Connaught Street - J.H. Beaton House – c. 1928 – Tudor style

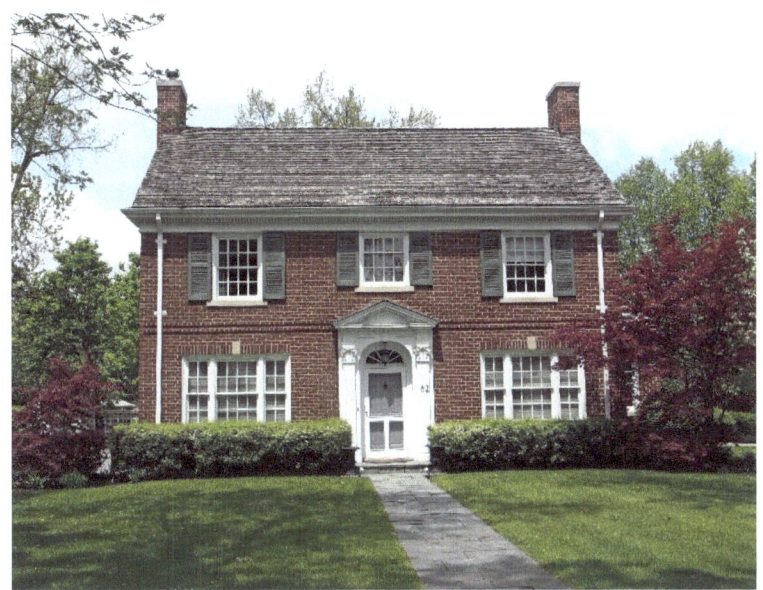

62 Connaught Street – 1923 – Georgian style

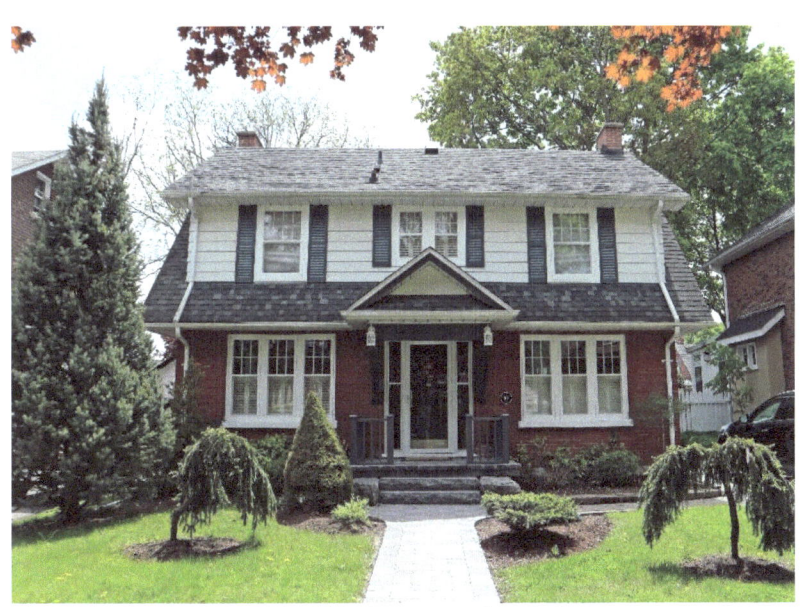

99 Connaught Street – shed dormer

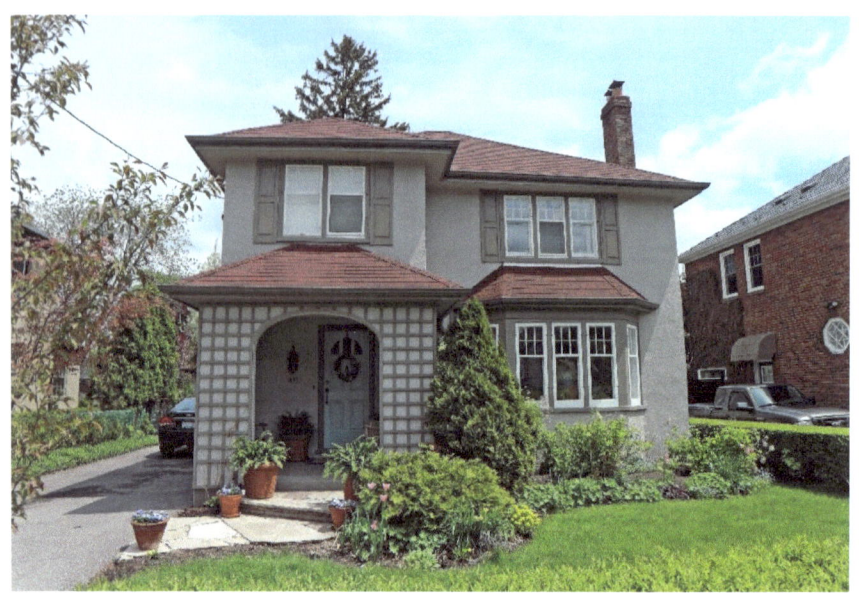

417 Mary Street North

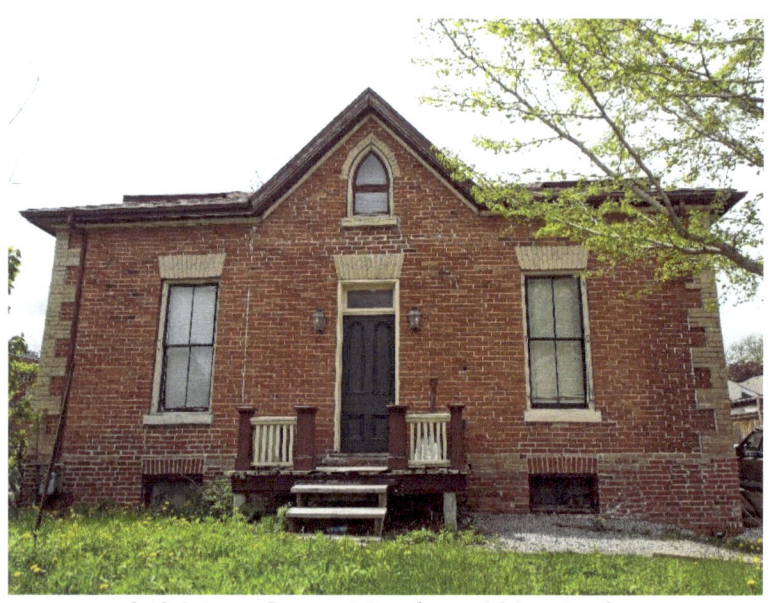

342 Mary Street North – 1920 - Gothic

Uxbridge, Ontario – Book 1 - in Colour Photos – My Top 9 Picks

Uxbridge is a township in the Regional Municipality of Durham in south-central Ontario and is located about forty kilometers northeast of Metropolitan Toronto. The main center in the township is the community of Uxbridge. Other communities within the township include Coppins Corners, Goodwood, Leaskdale, Sandford, Siloam, Victoria's Corner, and Zephyr.

It was named for Uxbridge, England, a name which was derived from "Wixan's Bridge".

The first settlers in the area were Quakers who started arriving in 1806 from Pennsylvania. The community's oldest building, the Uxbridge Friends Meeting House, was built in 1820 and overlooks the town from Quaker Hill, a kilometer to the west.

The first passenger-carrying narrow-gauge railway in North America, the Toronto and Nipissing Railway arrived in Uxbridge in June 1871, and for over a decade Uxbridge was the headquarters of the railway. In 1872, the Village of Uxbridge was separated from the Township and incorporated as a separate entity. With the creation of the Regional Municipality of Durham in 1974, Uxbridge Township was amalgamated with the Town of Uxbridge and Scott Township to create an expanded Township of Uxbridge.

Today, Uxbridge is as a mostly suburban community in northern Durham Region. Major manufacturing employers include Pine Valley Packaging (packaging, containers and portable shelters), Koch-Glitsch Canada (mass transfer systems) and Hela Canada (spice and ingredient manufacture). Many residents commute to other centers in Durham and York Regions and beyond.

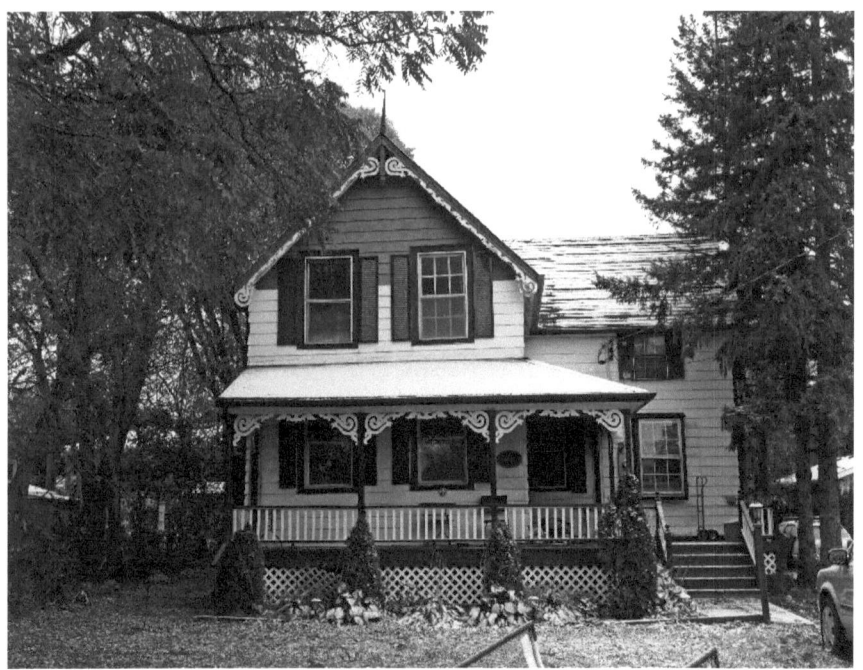

169 Brock Street West – Jones House – Town Constable – c. 1876 – Gothic Revival with verge board trim and finial on gable

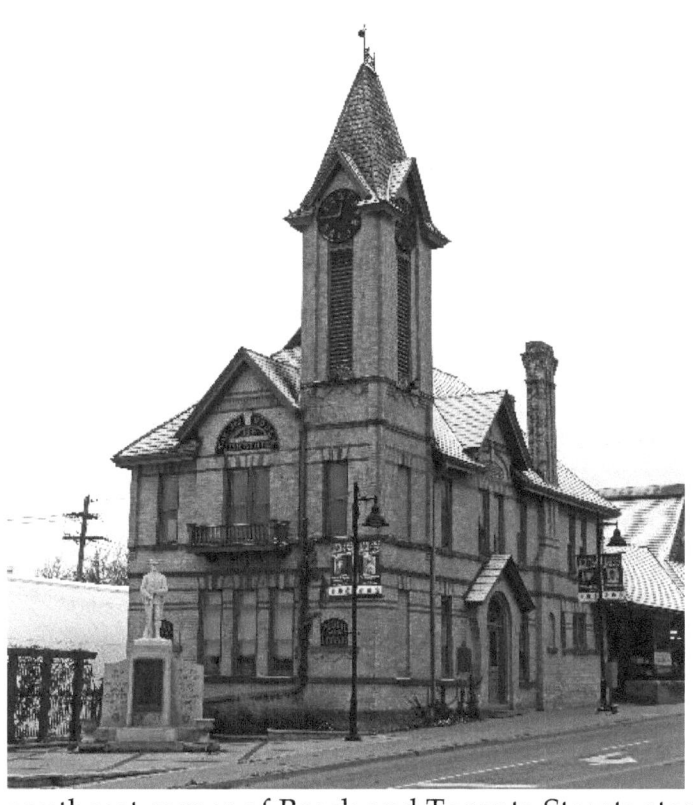

At the southeast corner of Brock and Toronto Streets stands the Uxbridge Public Library (c. 1887). It was beautifully restored in 1985. Uxbridge's citizen, Joseph Gould, commissioned it as a Mechanics' Institute and John T. Stokes of Sharon was the probable architect. It is in the High Victorian Gothic style of architecture which is reflected in its picturesque roofline, impressive clock tower and lavish attention to detail such as projecting brick courses, buttresses, bricks set in a diagonal pattern, decorative red brick, ornate chimneys and dropped brick keystones over the windows.

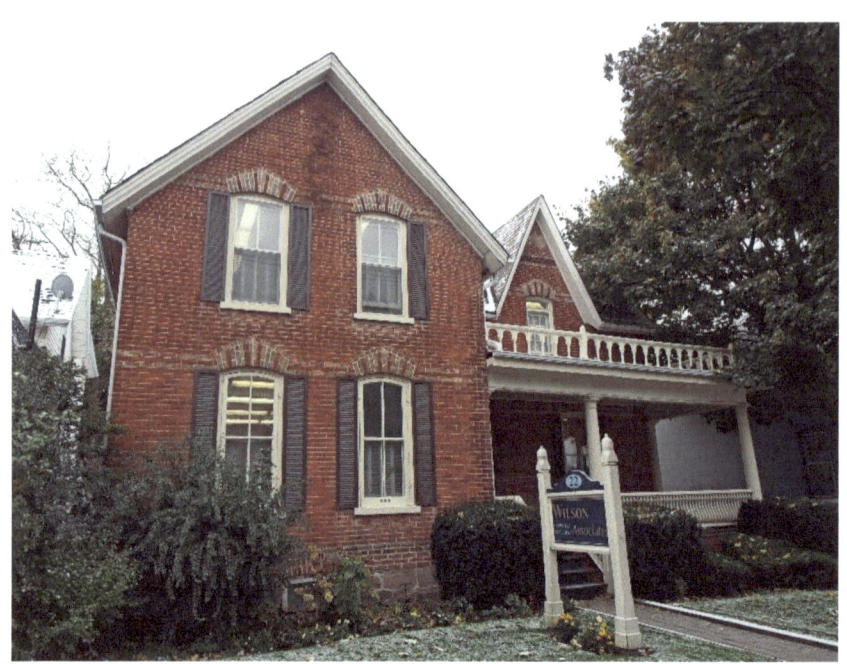

22 Brock Street East

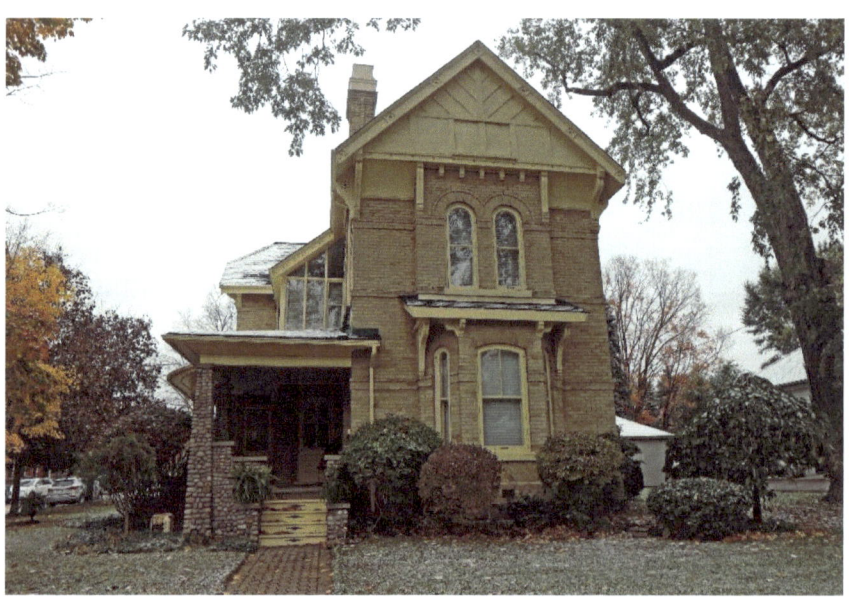

35 Brock Street East

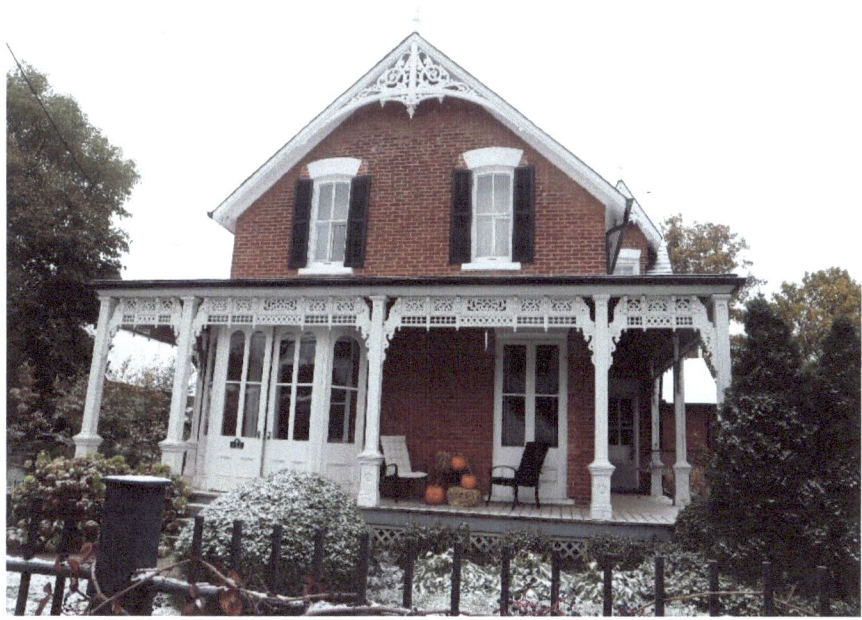

112 Brock Street East - This house was built in 1871 by Samuel Umphrey, a prominent Uxbridge Businessman, who played an important role in the Uxbridge Cabinet Organ Factory. This Victorian house has a fine example of bargeboard, spool work and fretwork.

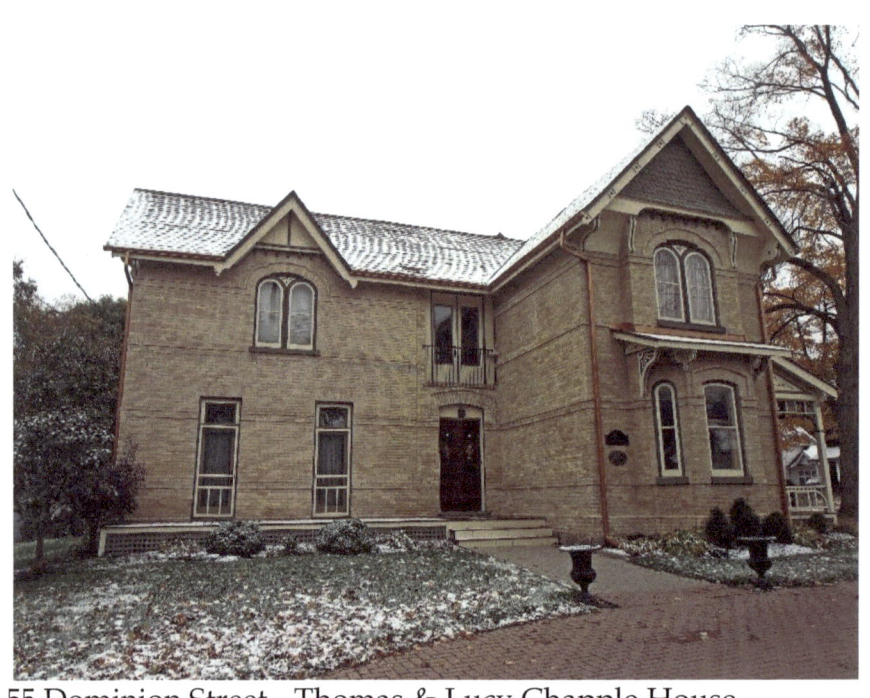

55 Dominion Street - Thomas & Lucy Chapple House, Barrister & MPP – c. 1885 – fish scale patterning in gable, decorative cornice and brackets, rounded double windows with voussoirs, banding

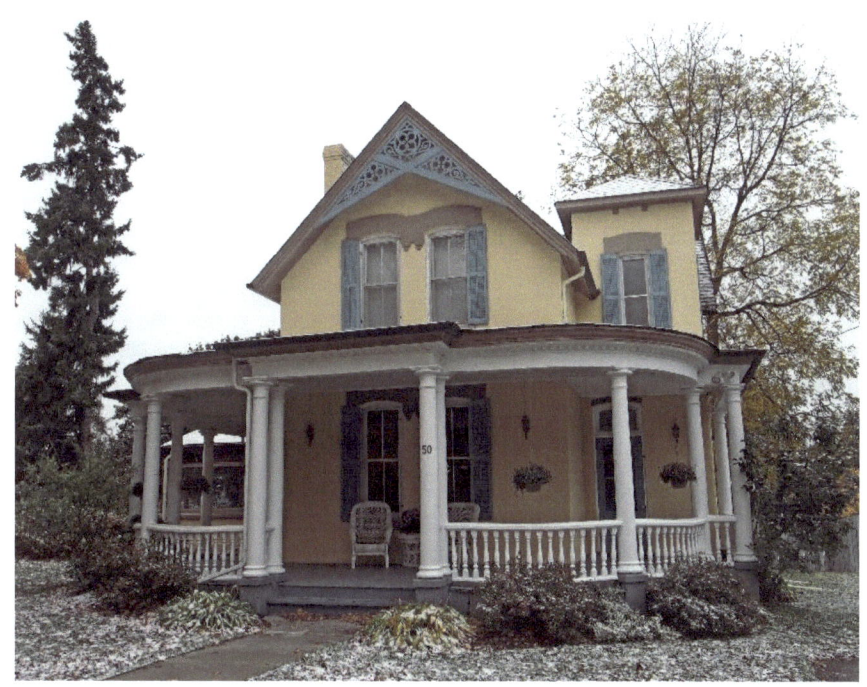

50 Dominion Street – wraparound verandah, verge board trim on gable, two-storey square tower

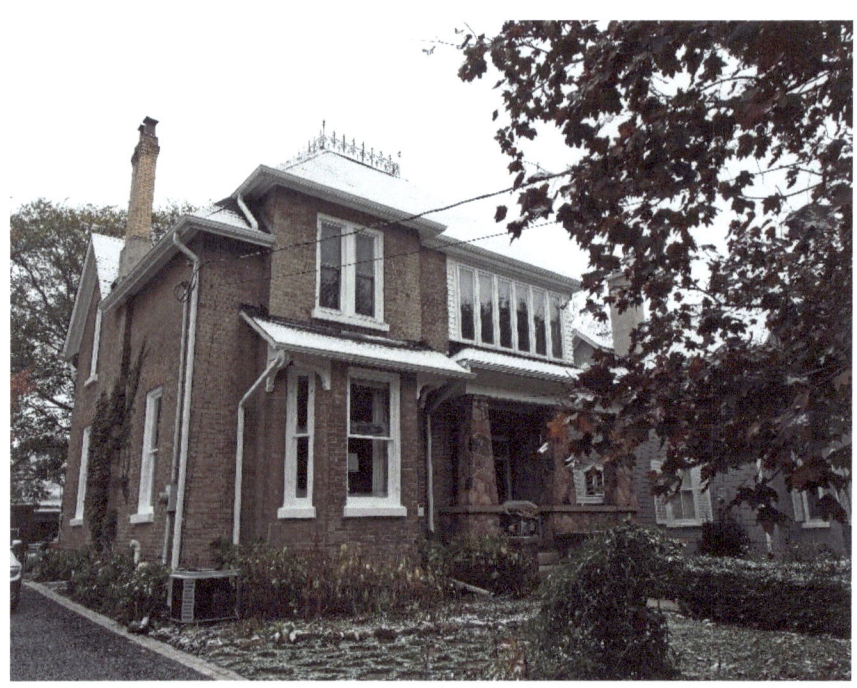

23 First Avenue - c. 1888 - David Thirsk (carpenter) purchased the lot in 1887 and built this Gothic Revival two-storey yellow bricked home with a coursed fieldstone basement. In 1908 it was purchased by W.H. Brownscombe who was in the Boot and Shoe business. There is a widow's walk with iron cresting on the rooftop.

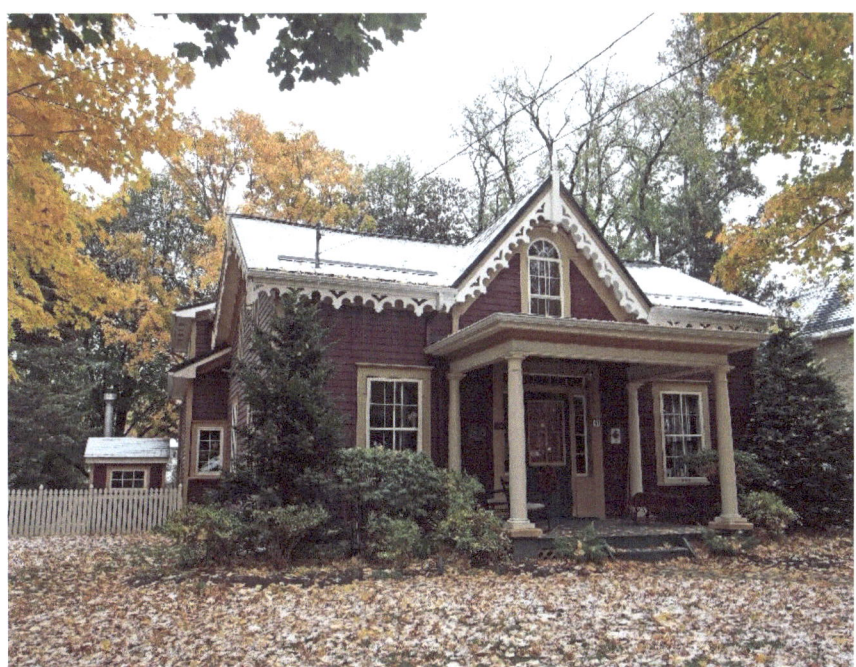

41 First Avenue - The 1½ storey Ontario Cottage style Wheler House was built in 1860 by Edward Wheler at the northwest corner of Brock and Main Street with the lumber coming from the local mill owned by George Wheler. It was moved to its present location by Ira G. Crosby in 1871. He was the Town Treasurer for many years.

Uxbridge, Ontario – Book 2 - in Colour Photos – My Top 11 Picks

Uxbridge is a township in the Regional Municipality of Durham in south-central Ontario and is located about forty kilometers northeast of Metropolitan Toronto. The main center in the township is the community of Uxbridge. Other communities within the township include Coppins Corners, Goodwood, Leaskdale, Sandford, Siloam, Victoria's Corner, and Zephyr.

The first settlers in the area were Quakers who started arriving in 1806 from Pennsylvania. The community's oldest building, the Uxbridge Friends Meeting House, was built in 1820 and overlooks the town from Quaker Hill, a kilometer to the west.

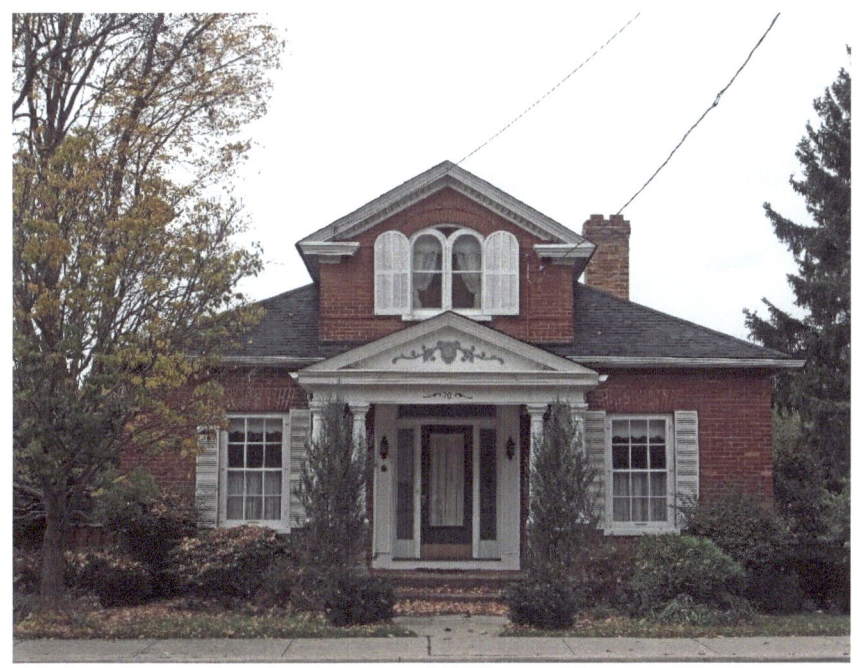

70 Main Street South - Bascom-Williams House - The house was a small square frame house that was later bricked. The property was originally owned by Dr. Joseph Bascom and was transferred to his daughter Mary in 1872. Mary married Alonzo D. Williams who was the first clerk for the Village of Uxbridge and held that position for 27 years.

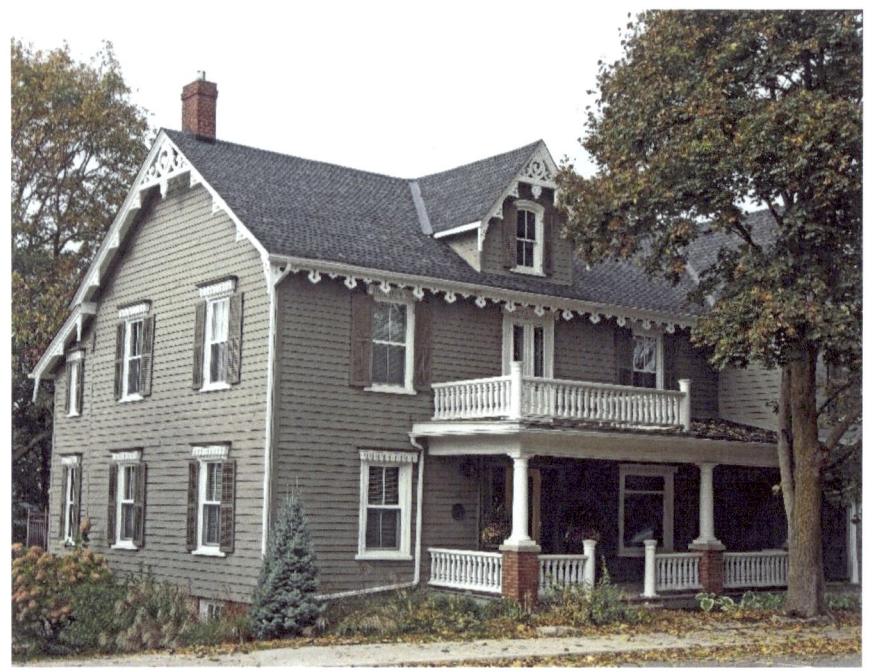

38 Main Street South - Dr. Mellow-Dr. Bascom House – c. 1863
– verge board trim on gables

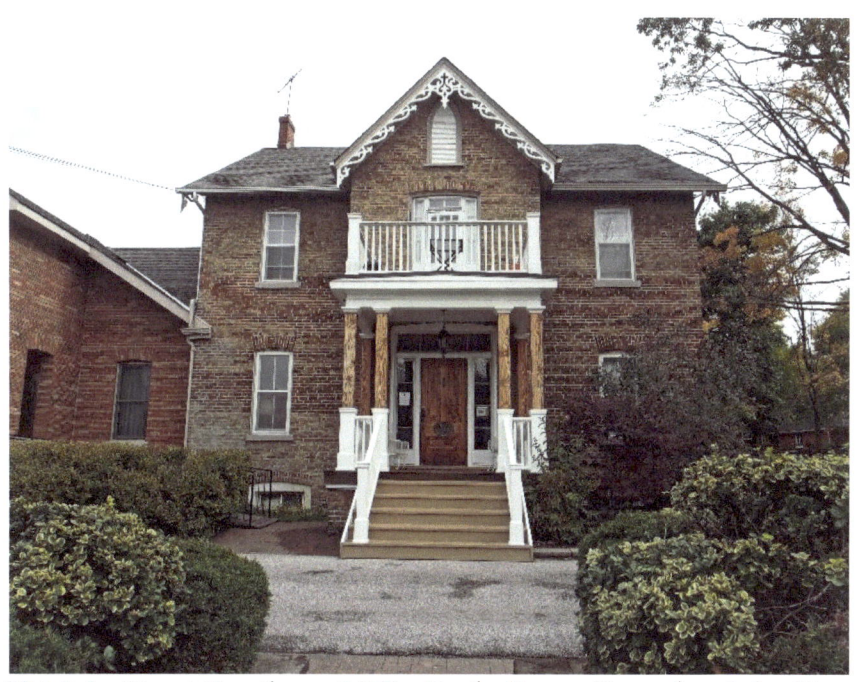

23 Main Street South - c. 1873 - Early Town Founder, John P. Plank bought 100 acres at the corner of Main and Brock Street in 1825. In 1828 he built the first store in Town and the first saw mill at Elgin Pond.

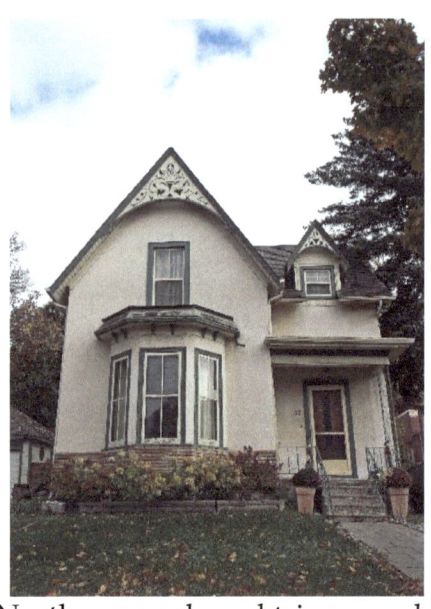

27 Main Street North - verge board trim on gables, bay window with brackets

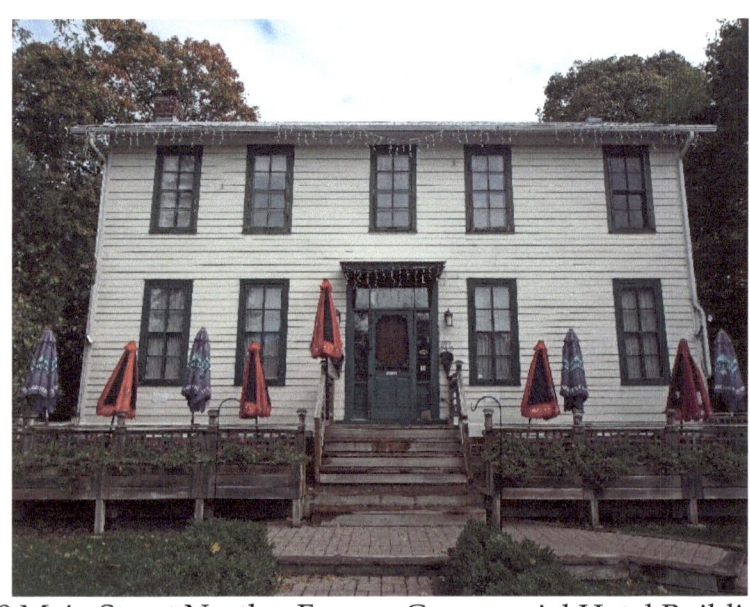

39 Main Street North – Former Commercial Hotel Building and Property - Hobby Horse Arms – c. 1868 – Georgian style

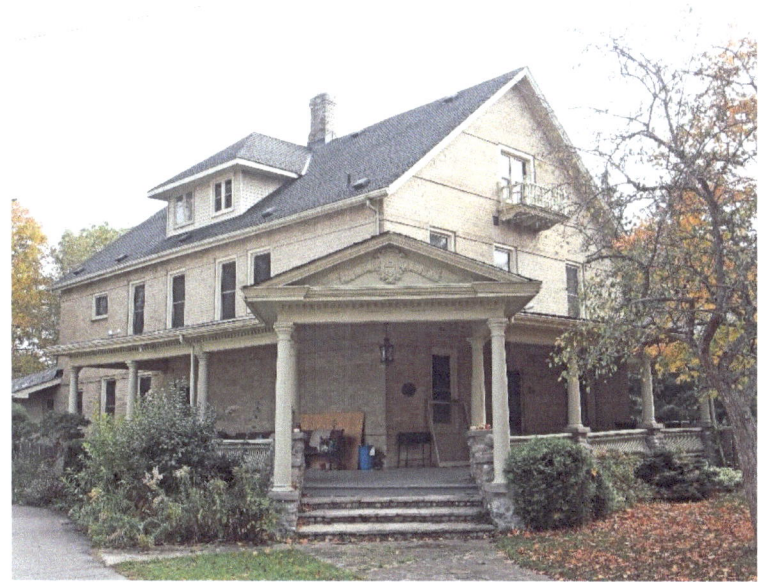

23 Franklin Street - Charles Small, Gleeholme, Owner of the Uxbridge Piano & Organ Company – c. 1901

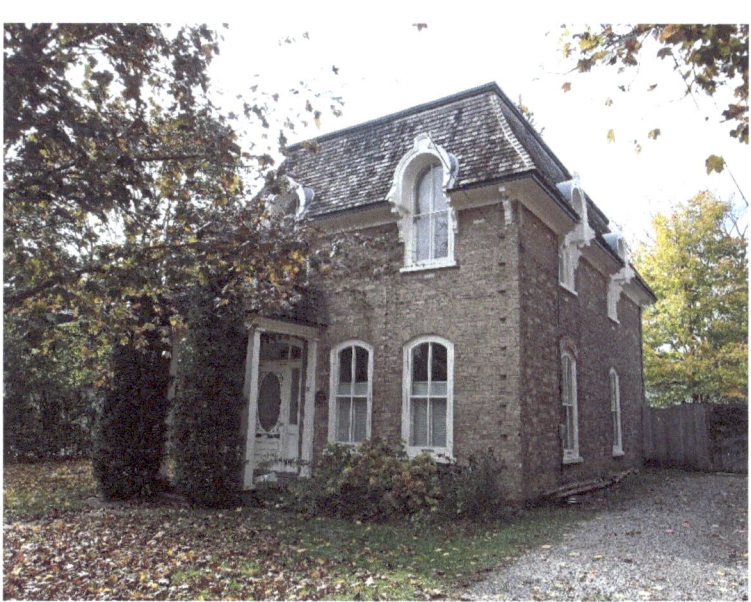

30 Franklin Street - Halbert Hardy House – A. S. Hardy, tuner – c. 1875 – Second Empire style - mansard roof, window hoods

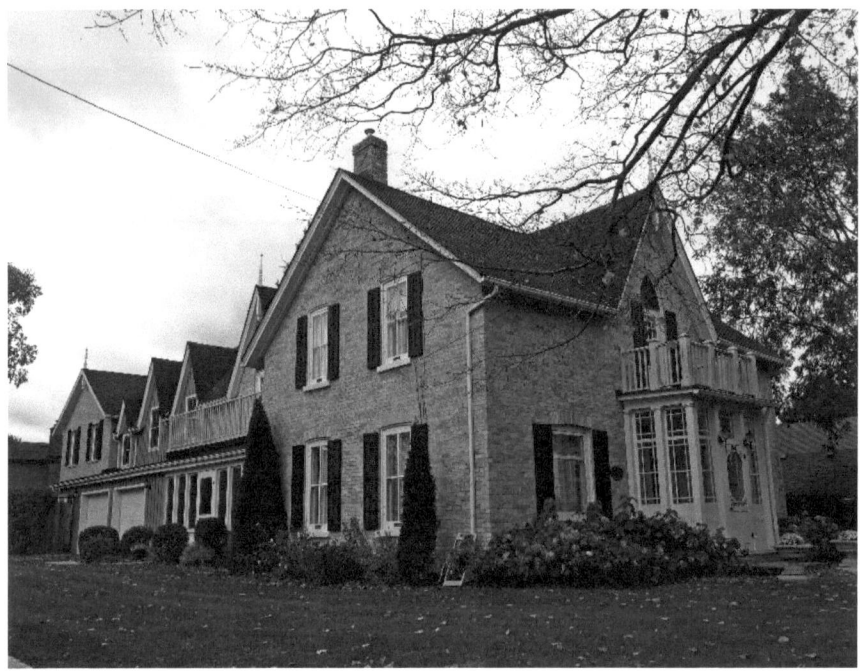

54 Cedar Street North - Harvey and Martha Gould House – c. 1877 - T-shaped 1½ storey white brick house built by Joseph Gould (merchant and miller). In 1886 it was purchased by Harvey Gould a former Mayor of Uxbridge, County Warden.

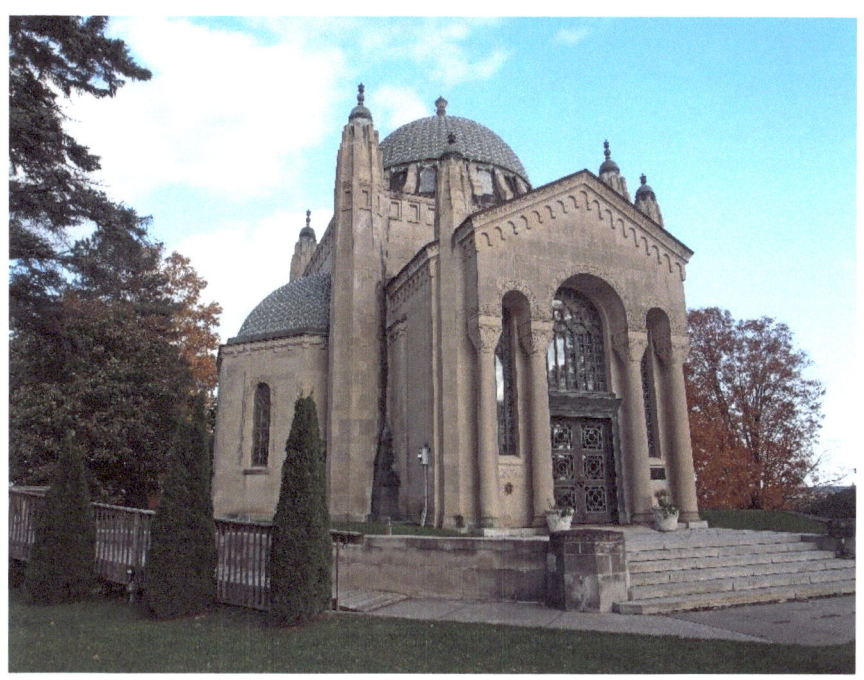

The Thomas Foster Memorial Temple, erected in 1935-36 by the former mayor of Toronto, is situated a short distance north of town. Inspired by Foster's visit to India, the Temple was designed by architects J.H. Craig (1889–1954) and H.H. Madrill (1889–1998).

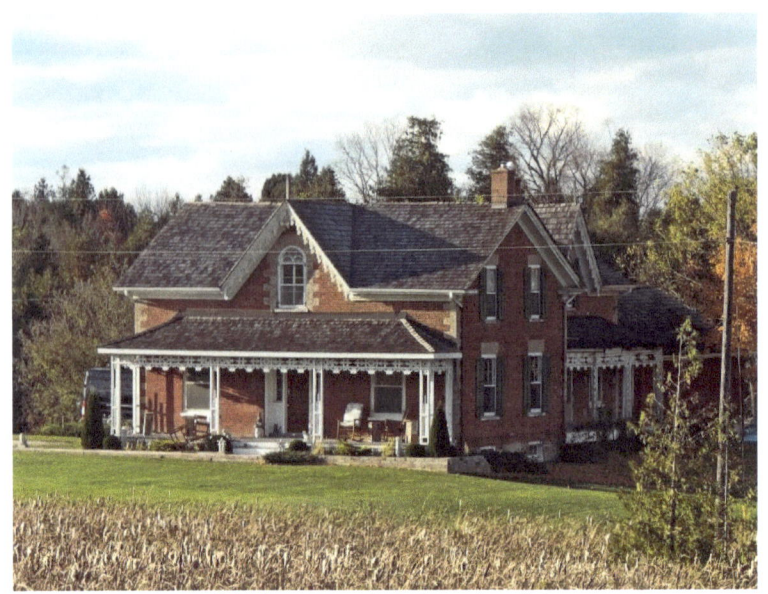

#690 – Leaskdale - Gothic

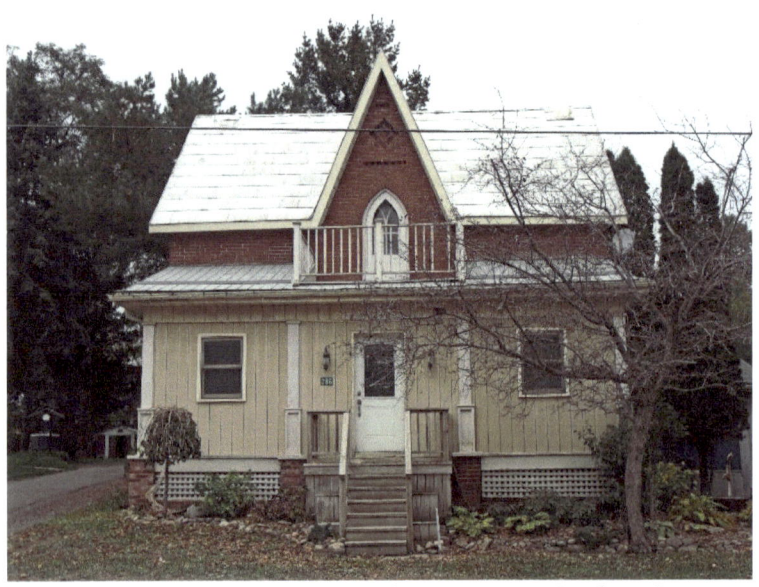

286 Highway 47, Goodwood – Ontario Gothic Cottage

Port Perry, Ontario in Colour Photos – My Top 10 Picks

Port Perry is a community located in Scugog, Ontario. The town is located northeast of Toronto and just north of Oshawa. The area around Port Perry was first surveyed as part of Reach Township by Major S. Wilmot in 1809. The first settler in the area was Reuben Crandell, a United Empire Loyalist who built a homestead with his wife in May 1821.

Settler Peter Perry laid out village lots on the shore of Lake Scugog in 1848 on the site of a former native village known as Scugog Village. The town site was named Port Perry in 1852 and its first Postmaster was Joseph Bigelow.

The first train on the Port Whitby and Port Perry Railway reached the terminus in Port Perry in 1872. Cargo from all over northern Ontario was shipped via the Trent-Severn Waterway to Port Perry via Lake Scugog, and then via the railway to Whitby, where it could be loaded onto the Canadian Pacific or Canadian National mainlines running along the shore of Lake Ontario, or onto ships in Port Whitby.

The village was amalgamated with Cartwright, Reach and Scugog Townships to form the Township of Scugog in 1974 upon the creation of the Regional Municipality of Durham.

On July 3, 1884 the entire business section of Port Perry was destroyed by fire. The wooden buildings exploded when sparks hit them. The Ross & Sons Grain Elevator on the waterfront, plus two other buildings were the only ones to survive. Thirty-three commercial buildings housing nearly fifty businesses, as well as factories, warehouses, stables, six lodges, and a dozen homes were reduced to rubble in under an hour. Four months later, the entire commercial sector with seventeen large brick buildings were built.

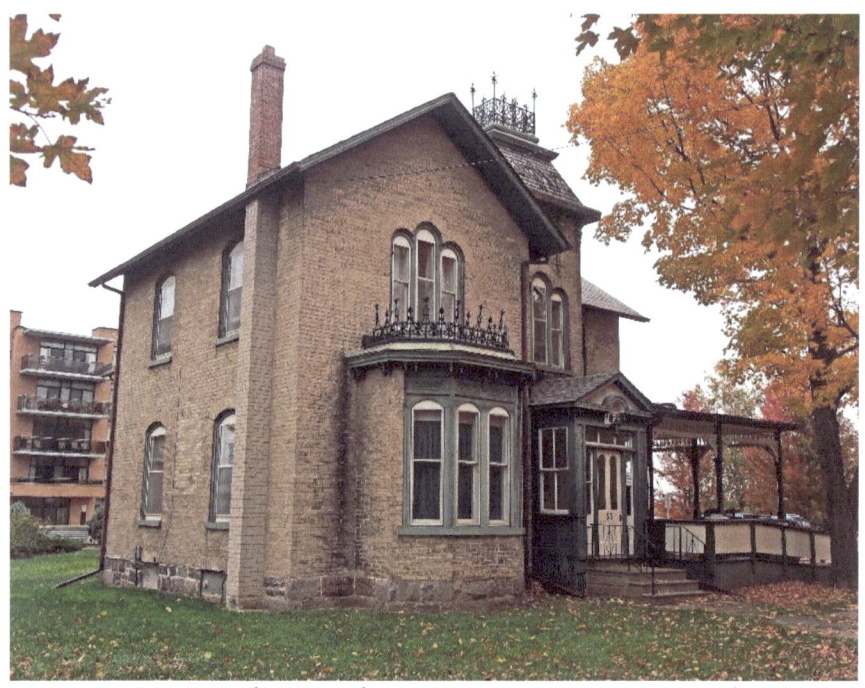

53 Perry Street - The Burnham House is a two-storey brick house that was built for John W. Burnham in 1878. The house is located on a large lot that overlooks Lake Scugog to the east. Mr. Burnham served as the local postmaster for 45 years.

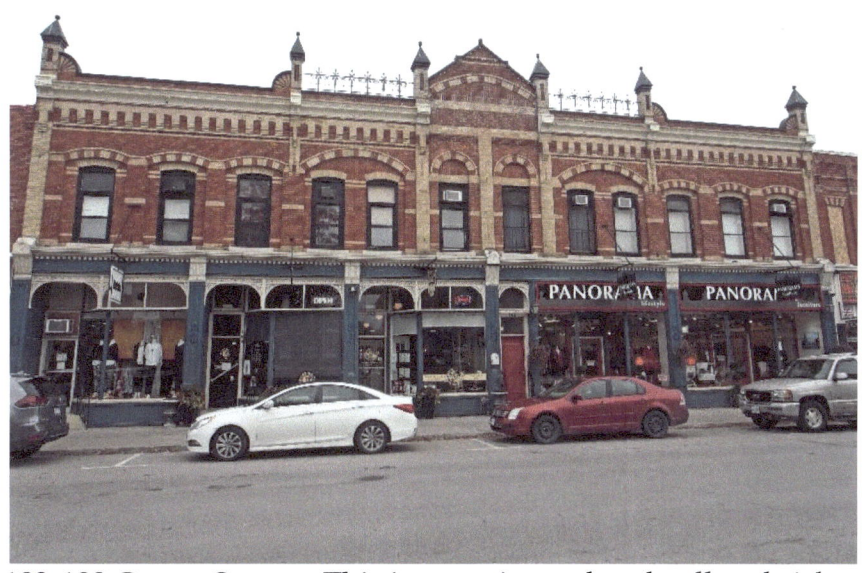

183-189 Queen Street – This impressive red and yellow brick building was constructed in 1885 by Jonathan Blong. He divided the building into a number of units which were leased to local shopkeepers.

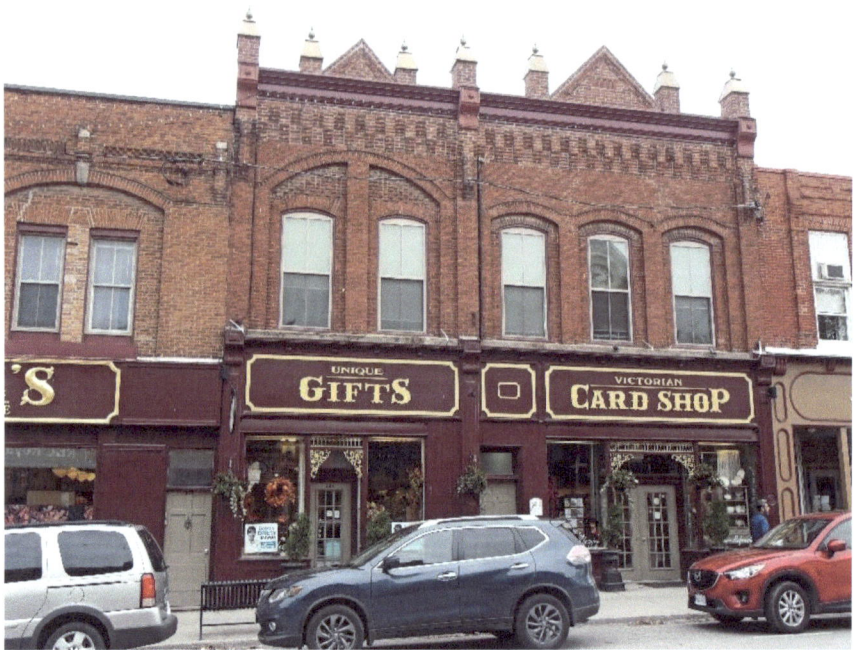

201-203 Queen Street – William Jones formed a partnership with John McClung when this new building was built after the fire destroyed the earlier building in 1884. Clothes, groceries, crockery, boots and shoes were sold. Charles Jones operated a dry goods store in the eastern part. In 1988 the property was purchased by Wayne and Carolyn Luke who opened the Victorian Card Shop in this section.

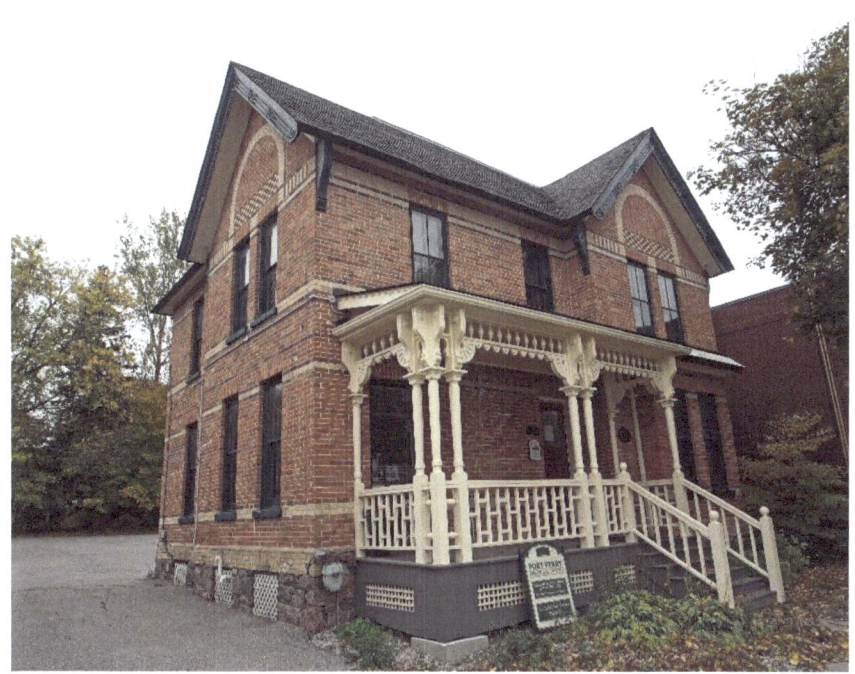

250 Queen Street – Dr. Orr Graham, a veterinarian, had this house built in 1886. Upon his retirement in 1909, he sold his house and practice to Dr. John T. Elliot. Dr. Coates arrived in 1910. In 2010, Michael and Frank Konopaski purchased the property and operate their business Scugog Financial and Scugog Accounting Professional Corporation.

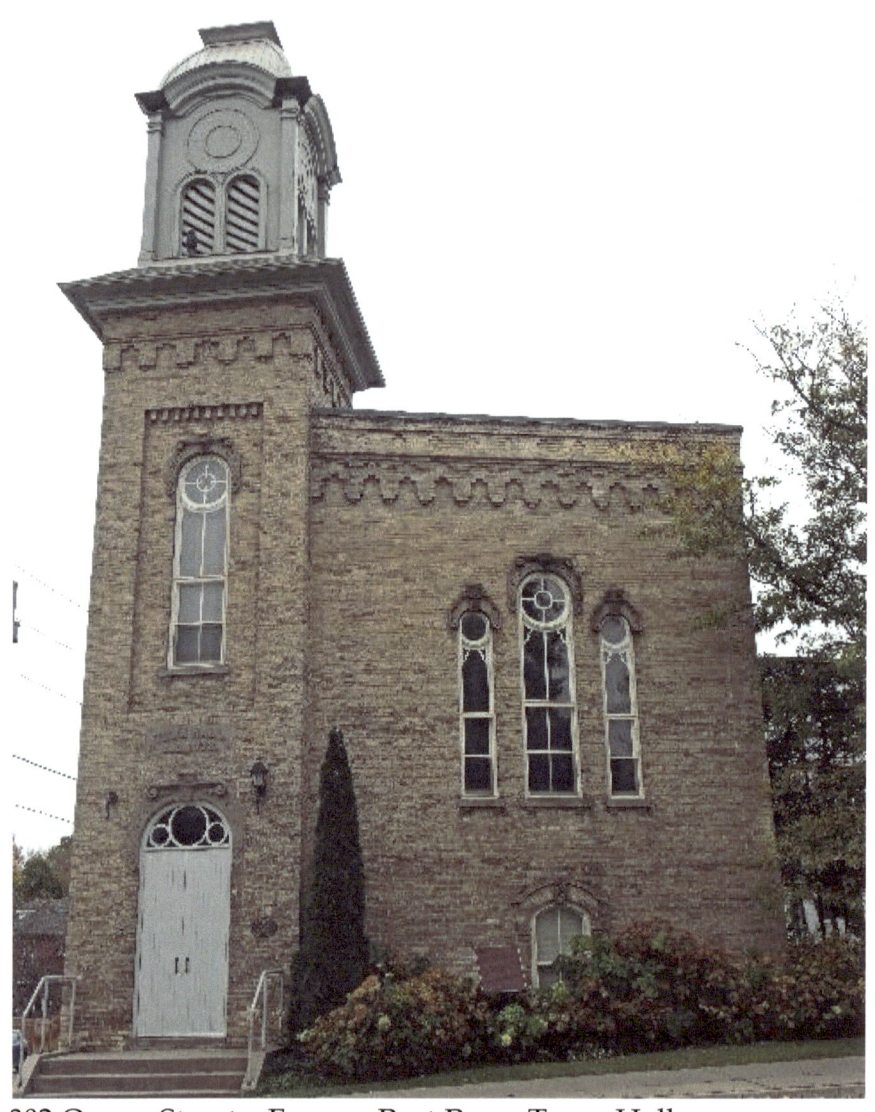

302 Queen Street – Former Port Perry Town Hall – Constructed in 1873, first project of Joseph Bigelow, the first Reeve of Port Perry. Many architectural features of Italianate style, reproduction of the original bell tower.

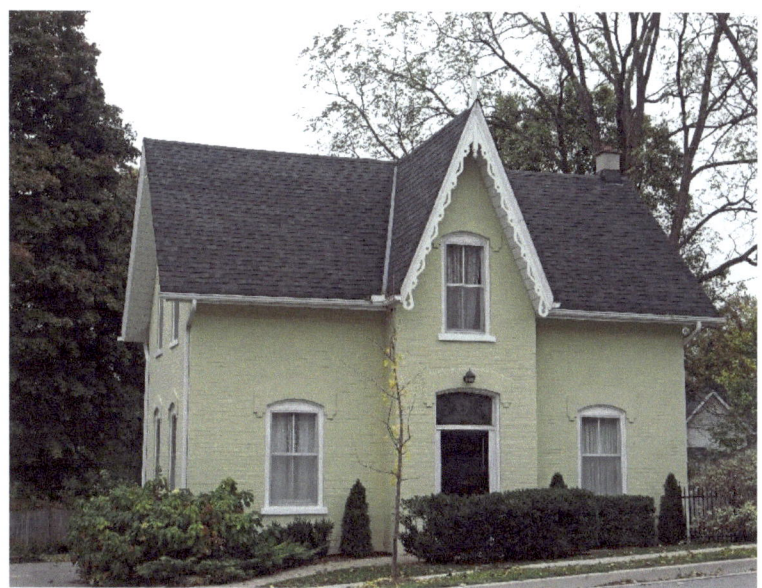

Queen Street – Gothic Revival - verge board trim and finial on gable

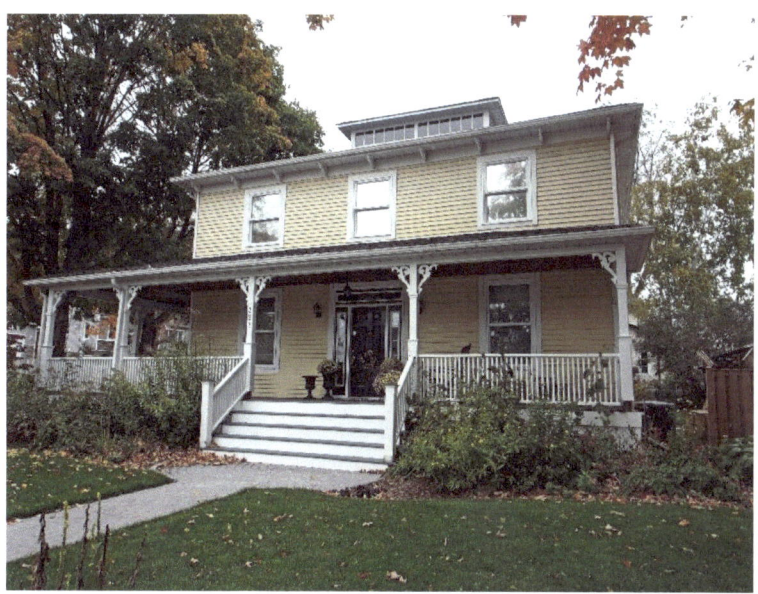

327 Queen Street – Dr. Richard Jones' residence – two storey, aluminum siding, belvedere on rooftop – c. 1897

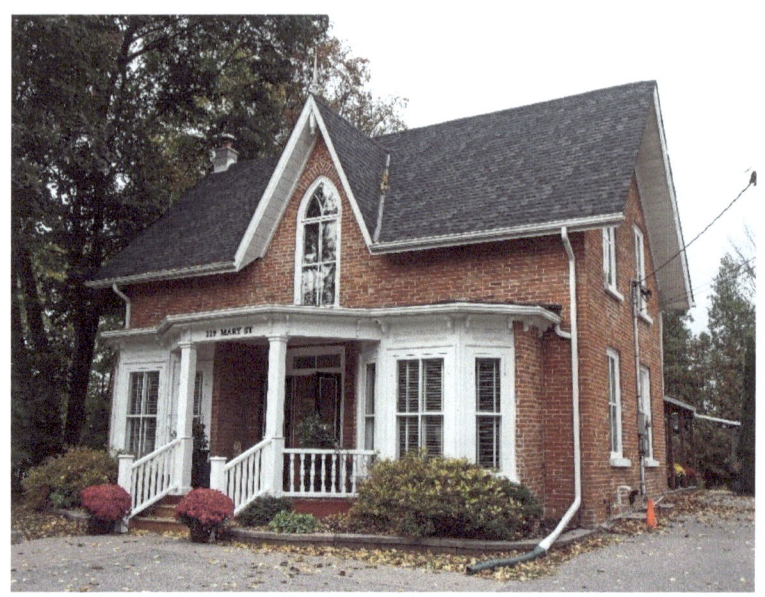

229 Mary Street – S.E. Allen Residence – 1½ storey, brick, Victorian Gothic, symmetrical center hall plan, c. 1870

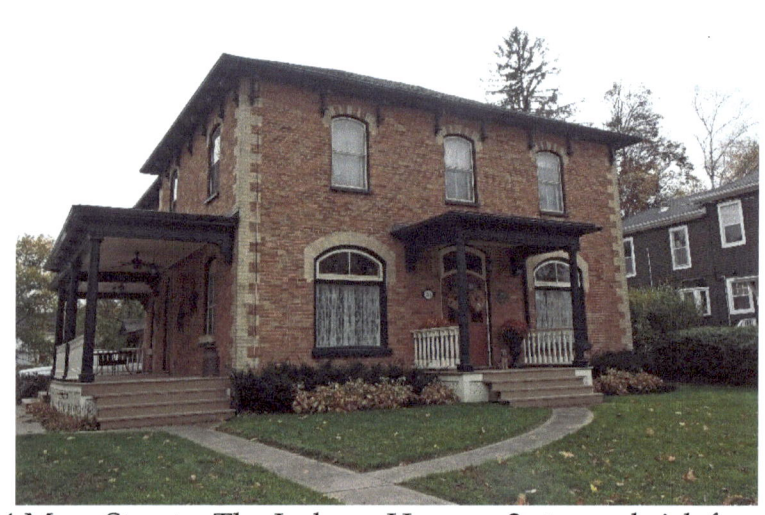

234 Mary Street – The Jackson House – 2 storey, brick façade, c. 1880

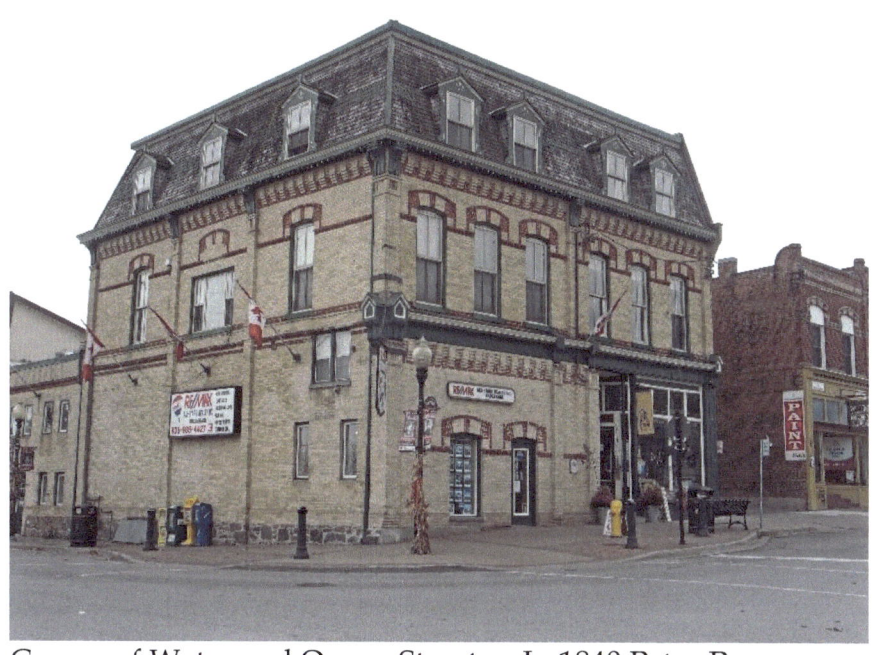

Corner of Water and Queen Streets – In 1840 Peter Perry purchased forty acres in downtown Port Perry and in 1844 he built a frame building which house a store, trading post, and a home for his agent, Chester Draper. Immediately after Perry's death is 1851, the property was bought by Mason and Phillips who turned it into a hotel. Henry Charles purchased it in 1867. The present yellow building was built after the fire of 1884. The hotel had thirty rooms including a dining room and at the street level were two stores including a sample room where salesmen could display their wares. They named it the St. Charles Hotel after Henry Charles.

www.ingramcontent.com/pod-product-compliance
Lightning Source LLC
Chambersburg PA
CBHW041104180526
45172CB00001B/103